DISTANCE L

MW00800152

FEATURED ARTICLES

EDITOR
Michael Simonson
simsmich@nova.edu

MANAGING EDITOR
Charles Schlosser
cschloss@nova.edu

ASSISTANT EDITOR
Anymir Orellana
orellana@nova.edu

EDITORIAL ASSISTANT
Khitam Azaiza
azaiza@nova.edu

COLLEGE EDITOR
Eunice Luyegu
eluyegu@nova.edu

ASSOCIATION EDITOR
John G. Flores
jflores@usdla.org

PUBLISHER
Information Age Publishing
11600 North Community
  House Road, Ste. 250
Charlotte, NC 28277
(704) 752-9125
(704) 752-9113 Fax
www.infoagepub.com

ADVERTISING
United States Distance
  Learning Association
76 Canal Street, Suite 301

Boston, MA 02114
617-399-1770, x11

EDITORIAL OFFICES
Fischler College of Education
Nova Southeastern
  University
3301 College Ave.
Fort Lauderdale, FL 33314
954-262-8563
FAX 954-262-3724
simsmich@nova.edu

PURPOSE
Distance Learning, an official publication of the United States Distance Learning Association (USDLA), is sponsored by the USDLA, by the Fischler College of Education at Nova Southeastern University, and by Information Age Publishing. Distance Learning is published four times a year for leaders, practitioners, and decision makers in the fields of distance learning, e-learning, telecommunications, and related areas. It is a professional magazine with information for those who provide instruction to all types of learners, of all ages, using telecommunications technologies of all types. Articles are written by practitioners for practitioners with the intent of providing usable information and ideas for readers. Articles are accepted from authors with interesting and important information about the effective practice of distance teaching and learning.

SPONSORS
The United States Distance Learning (USDLA) is the professional organization for those involved in distance teaching and learning. USDLA is committed to being the leading distance learning association in the United States. USDLA serves the needs of the distance learning community by providing advocacy, information, networking and opportunity. www.usdla.org

NSU's College of Health Care Sciences (CHCS) is the place where compassion and health care meet. At CHCS, the ability to help patients and communities begins with specialized skills developed in our undergraduate, graduate, professional, and postprofessional programs. The demand for health care specialists has never been greater, and CHCS students get a competitive edge in our high-tech clinical simulation labs and surgical suites, which create a real feel for what they will face in the health care profession.

Students in CHCS learn from experienced faculty members who practice what they teach in the health care professions, including anesthesiology, audiology, cardiopulmonary sciences, health sciences, health and human performance, occupational therapy, physician assistant, physical therapy, and speech-language pathology. CHCS programs are conveniently offered on campus and in blended formats.
CHCS—NSU
3200 S. University Drive
Ft. Lauderdale, FL 33328

877-640-0218
http://healthsciences.nova.edu

INFORMATION AGE PUBLISHING
11600 North Community House Road, Ste. 250
Charlotte, NC 28277
(704) 752-9125
(704) 752-9113 Fax
www.infoagepub.com

SUBSCRIPTIONS
Members of the United States Distance Learning Association receive *Distance Learning* as part of their membership. Others may subscribe to *Distance Learning*.
Individual Subscription: $60
Institutional Subscription: $150
Student Subscription: $40

DISTANCE LEARNING RESOURCE INFORMATION:
Visit http://www.usdla.org/html/resources/dlmag/index.htm
Advertising Rates and Information:
617-399-1770, x11
Subscription Information:
Contact USDLA at
617-399-1770
info@usdla.org

DISTANCE LEARNING
is indexed by the Blended, Online Learning and Distance Education (BOLDE) research bank.

DISTANCE LEARNING MAGAZINE
SPONSORED BY THE
U.S. DISTANCE LEARNING ASSOCIATION,
COLLEGE OF HEALTH CARE SCIENCES,
NOVA SOUTHEASTERN UNIVERSITY
AND INFORMATION AGE PUBLISHING

MANUSCRIPT PREPARATION GUIDELINES

Articles are accepted from authors with interesting and important information about the effective practice of distance teaching and learning. No page costs are charged authors, nor are stipends paid. Two copies of the issue with the author's article will be provided. Reprints will also be available.

1. Manuscripts should be written in Microsoft Word, saved as a .doc file or docx file, and sent on flash drive or CD.

2. *Single* space the entire manuscript. Use 12 point Times New Roman (TNR) font.

3. Laser print two copies of the paper.

4. Margins: 1" on all sides.

5. Do not use any page numbers or embedded commands. Documents that have embedded commands will be returned.

6. Include a cover sheet with the paper's title and with the names, affiliations and addresses of all authors. High-resolution professional photographs of all authors should be included and should have a file size larger than 500kb.

7. Submit the paper on a flash drive or CD that is clearly marked. The name of the manuscript file should reference the author. In addition, submit two paper copies. Send the digital and paper copies to:

Michael R. Simonson
Editor
Distance Learning journal
Fischler College of Education
Nova Southeastern University

3301 College Avenue
Fort Lauderdale, FL 33314
simsmich@nova.edu

The Manuscript

Word Processor Format
Manuscripts should be written in Microsoft Word.

Length
There is no mandatory length. The average manuscript is between 3,000 and 5,000 words.

Text
Regular text: 12 point TNR, left justified

Paper title: 14 point TNR, centered

Author listing: 12 point TNR, centered

Section headings: 12 point TNR, centered

Section subheading: 12 point TNR, left justified

Do not type section headings or titles in all-caps, only capitalize the first letter in each word. All type should be single-spaced. Allow one line of space before and after each heading. Indent, 0.5", the first sentence of each paragraph.

Figures and Tables
Figures and tables should fit width 6 ½" and be incorporated into the document.

Page Numbering
Do not include or refer to any page numbers in your manuscript.

Graphics
We encourage you to use visuals—pictures, graphics, charts—to help explain your article. Graphics images (.jpg) should be included at the end of your paper. Graphic images should be at least 500 kb in size.

Perfect Storm for the Quality Course Review at UCF

Aimee deNoyelles, Amanda Major, Denise Lowe,
Tina Calandrino, and Alyssa Albrecht

INTRODUCTION

Can anyone easily define "quality" in online courses? Is it a nebulous term that is just a marketing ploy to attract students, or are there standards and precedents set for a common understanding? Current online courses are now considered as much of traditional higher education as brick and mortar face-to-face instruction; in fact, online learning has expanded to the point that a student from one state can get a full degree online offered from a higher education institution located in another state. Students within the Florida State University System can take online classes from multiple institutions within Florida and earn one degree. The flexibility and choice is great in some aspects, but it can make institutions nervous regarding enrollments and retention. What if students start enrolling in classes at another university because the reputation

Aimee deNoyelles,
Instructional Design Team Lead, Personnel Management, Center for Distributed Learning, University of Central Florida, 4000 Central Florida Blvd., LIB-107, Orlando, FL 32816-2810. Telephone: (407) 823-1675. E-mail: aimee.denoyelles@ucf.edu

Amanda Major,
Instructional Designer, Center for Distributed Learning, University of Central Florida, 4000 Central Florida Blvd., LIB-107, Orlando, FL 32816-2810. Telephone: (407) 823-4929. E-mail: Amanda.Major@ucf.edu

is deemed "better"—or perhaps more troubling—"easier"? Often students choose to enroll in online higher education based on the brand recognition of the institution. For online college students, the top three most important factors in choosing which school to enroll, behind tuition and fees, are the reputation of the program and school as reported most frequently by Clinefelter and Aslanian in 2017. Nevertheless, quality online courses are increasingly difficult to distinguish. Some universities with excellent brands use no quality assurance system or employ outside organizations and faculty to contribute to components of their online learning programs. If the programs and courses do not live up to an institution's reputation, then students, because of the proliferation of options, have a greater opportunity than ever to choose a different online offering, literally, with a click of a mouse. As a mechanism for upholding the mission of the University of Central Florida (UCF) and its stellar reputation for delivering quality online and hybrid courses, UCF began a quality initiative. The aim was to verify that online courses at UCF met standards for quality, informed by best practices and nationally recognized quality course standards.

BACKGROUND: "QUALITY" IN ONLINE COURSES

QUALITY IN THE LITERATURE

In the past, measuring quality within the educational literature was primarily achieved by comparing online course data to that of face-to-face courses. Doing so assumes the premise that face-to-face courses set the standards in which to be compared, which is not necessarily the case (Mitchell, 2010). More recently, quality in online education has been often measured in two ways: student data (satisfaction ratings and attrition), and adherence to course design standards and process (Lenert & Janes, 2017).

Online courses contain many components and often vary from each other

Denise Lowe,
Instructional Design Team Lead, Strategic Initiatives, Center for Distributed Learning, University of Central Florida, 4000 Central Florida Blvd., LIB-107, Orlando, FL 32816-2810. Telephone: (407) 823-4272.
E-mail: Denise.Lowe@ucf.edu

Tina Calandrino,
Instructional Designer, Center for Distributed Learning, University of Central Florida, 4000 Central Florida Blvd., LIB-107, Orlando, FL 32816-2810. Telephone: (407) 823-2838.
E-mail: Tina.Calandrino@ucf.edu

greatly, resulting in a lack of consensus on what constitutes a "quality" online course (Thompson, 2008). Several companies have arisen to take on the massive task of creating standards that model quality. Although there are differences between the companies' evaluations, the standards are similar overall and generally focus on best practices (Baldwin, Ching, & Hsu, 2017). There is some evidence in the literature to suggest that building a course using nationally recognized standards results in higher student perceptions (Crews, Bordonana, & Wilkinson, 2017) and overall improvement of online courses (Baldwin et al., 2017). It is important to note that the implementation of the standards is key. For instance, Bowser, Davis, Singleton, and Small (2017) implemented a five-phase collaborative review process to improve course development and delivery which involved multiple stakeholders. Professors self-assessed the quality of their course using Quality Matters standards, and peer-reviewed others' courses. Recommendations for revisions were made at a department level.

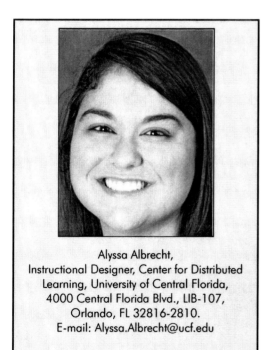

Alyssa Albrecht,
Instructional Designer, Center for Distributed Learning, University of Central Florida, 4000 Central Florida Blvd., LIB-107, Orlando, FL 32816-2810.
E-mail: Alyssa.Albrecht@ucf.edu

This collaborative process improved the quality of online programs within the college and has been designated as a "best practice" in the education field.

These findings suggest that reviewing a course for quality should result in a better online course to enhance both faculty and student satisfaction, as well as student learning outcomes.

It is important to note that there is not one magic factor that defines a quality experience. When measuring quality assurance strategies, "administrative leadership and support, ongoing program concerns, course development, student concerns and needs, and faculty development" should all be considered (Lee & Dziuban, 2002).

COURSE REVIEWS

The purpose of conducting quality reviews is to assess whether a course meets a set of standards from which quality can be judged. This set of standards can be utilized by experts in online course design and teaching as a standard to judge course quality across institutions. When a course meets quality standards, not only does this justify that the rigor of online courses compare to face-to-face courses, but it also provides professional development to those (faculty members and instructional designers, perhaps) contributing to the course production process. Those participants share with each other best practices for and trends in course design and delivery, which can impact practices beyond just the online course. From participation in course review processes, a large majority of participants either had enhanced or planned to enhance their online courses, as well as face-to-face courses (MarylandOnline, Inc., 2017b). Both the awareness of quality criteria and participation in the review of quality course criteria raise the quality of not solely online, but also the face-to-face curriculum.

The University of Maryland was one of the first to create and popularize a quality course review process for reviewing online and blended courses. The small group of colleagues in the MarlyandOnline, Inc. consortium successfully launched Quality Matters with grant funds to develop a method for assessing the quality of a course across modalities or course origination through training peer reviewers and conducting course reviews nationally (MarylandOnline, Inc., 2017a). The group received a grant to fund the implementation of their goal. Quality Matters persists today as scalable quality assurance programs with quality rubrics, derived from literature reviews about online learning and best practices of course developers and instructors.

The Quality Matters quality assurance systems encompass just a few of the many quality review systems available. Many other quality systems, usually encompassing a rubric and a course review process, emerged that focus specifically on online course design quality (e.g., State University of New York, Open SUNY Center for Online Teaching Excellence's *The Open SUNY COTE Quality Review Process and Rubric*, California State University's *Quality Online Learning and Teaching*, and University of Florida's *Standards and Markers of Excellence Review Form); some specifically focus on blended or e-learning courses rather than fully online courses (e.g., Center for Distributed Learning Blendkit Course's *Blended Course Self-assessment/Peer-review Form*, New Mexico State University's *Online Course Design Rubric*); and others focus on quality delivery of instruction (e.g., Online Learning Consortium's *Quality Course Teaching and Instructional Practice Scorecard* and California State University's *Rubric for Online Instruction*). Although various assessments are available to review quality components, the quality assurance system at UCF focuses on quality course design in higher education.

FOUNDATIONS OF ONLINE QUALITY AT UCF

Since its inception in 1995, with the very first online course offered a year later, UCF has invested in online learning to ensure quality in the course development process and outcomes. Early efforts to create a community of online faculty was accomplished through faculty development training (IDL6543) and the *Pegasus Connections*, "a compilation of resources for faculty and students which contained numerous tutorials.... Students [faculty participants] were able to use the disc to learn new skills, improve existing skills, or check their knowledge" (Truman, Futch, Thompson, & Yonekura, 1999).

Though IDL6543 has been redesigned a few times to remain current in content and design, its focus continues to engage participants on three principal tenets of quality: pedagogy, technology, and support (see Figure 1). While the Center for Distributed Learning (CDL) at UCF has many support teams to provide technical and course production assistance for faculty, the relationship between the faculty and instructional designers is the primary mechanism for developing quality courses. Other professional development opportunities are offered to faculty as well, in efforts to provide best practices for quality online course development, to include targeted topical formats such as faculty seminars in online teaching.

The issue of quality course development has historically been addressed in the training process through the course content, small groups, student and faculty panels, and the instructional design consultations. It appears to have paid off—students and faculty involved with online and blended courses at UCF have consistently reflected high satisfaction rates as found by Dziuban and Moskal (2016; see Appendix A). The researchers also found higher student success rates and lower rates of withdrawal when comparing online and blended courses to their traditional face-to-

IDL6543 Strategy

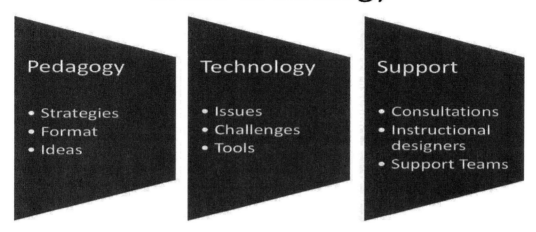

Figure 1.   Principal tenets of IDL6543.

face counterparts (Dziuban & Moskal, 2017; see Appendix B).

Although this research supports the idea that most faculty are already developing courses of quality design, the relationship forged with the instructional designer during IDL6543 is not always sustained once the participant completes the program. It has primarily been the faculty member's responsibility to reach out when needed, but instructors can teach without supervision or guidance if they so choose. The next step in promoting quality for UCF is creating a systematic method to guide optimal course design over the years through a course review process, while continuing to build relationships with faculty in a proactive and deliberate manner—a critical aspect of this initiative. Professional development programs, such as IDL6543, will embed the quality course process within the program itself, along with existing online course award programs, such as, Chuck D. Dziuban Award for Excellence in Online Teaching. This will create formal opportunities to incorporate specific processes that designate online courses as quality or high quality to effectively reach the goals of the SACS Accreditation, State University System 2025 Strategic Plan for Online Education, and the UCF Collective Impact Strategic Plan. These plans and commitments share a unifying goal—identifying quality online courses—and have resulted in CDL Strategic Initiatives with core components focused on faculty development and quality (see Figure 2).

QUALITY COURSE REVIEW PROCESS AT UCF

A quality initiative began at UCF to identify and implement strategies that would contribute to enhanced online courses, the primary strategy being the establishment of a course review process. To accomplish this, a task force of instructional designers reviewed several nationally recognized quality rubrics: Quality Matters, Quality Online Learning and Teaching, California State University Chico Rubric for Online Instruction, Open SUNY COTE Quality Review, along with a review and incorporation of existing UCF course standards used for credentialing faculty to teach online. The task force developed several iterations of the Quality Online Course Review (QORC), while carefully considering the applicability of the items and the

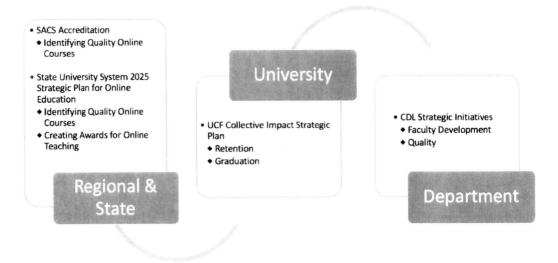

- SACS Accreditation
  - ◆ Identifying Quality Online Courses

- State University System 2025 Strategic Plan for Online Education
  - ◆ Identifying Quality Online Courses
  - ◆ Creating Awards for Online Teaching

Regional & State

University

- UCF Collective Impact Strategic Plan
  - ◆ Retention
  - ◆ Graduation

- CDL Strategic Initiatives
  - ◆ Faculty Development
  - ◆ Quality

Department

Figure 2. Relevant factors impacting the Quality Online Course Review Process.

culture of faculty across departments. To verify the instrument, the QOCR was compared to the essential standards of the Quality Matters Higher Education rubric, and it was modified to address the full intent of those Quality Matters essential items. Within 6 months of the initiation of the Quality Initiative, the enhancements from the iterations and Quality Matters crosswalk enhancements confirmed the QOCR rubric as equitable to nationally recognized standards of quality (see Appendix C).

Cross-functional support was sought from CDL to standardize and scale the course review process. An instructional designer created an instrument for ease of scoring and explaining the QOCR items during a quality course review, and a developer modified an existing database for documenting the process. The task force sought the expertise of technical support staff to expand their current role to include key course development efforts for assisting faculty with revising their courses to meet quality standards, as the intent is for all courses reviewed to ultimately meet QOCR's quality designation. Simultaneously, task force members collaborated

with graphic designers and developers to develop a badging system to designate courses as having met quality standards, which would enable the placement of a time- and date-stamped logo in online courses representing quality. With a quality process standardized, support for course development in place, and faculty champions, the QOCR process will continually improve and facilitate course improvement across the University as it grows in popularity, as an established scalable and sustainable quality course design assurance system at UCF.

COMMUNICATION PLANS

INSTRUCTORS

Communication with instructors is a critical component to the successful rollout of the course review process (Table 1). From the beginning, it was stressed that instructors would have the chance to review and have input into the review instrument. Once the QOCR was initially drafted, it was presented to a group of instructors who attended a campus conference session about quality in online courses. In the session, they were provided details about the state's strategic plan and given some time to ask the questions that immediately came to mind for them (for instance, "Is this mandatory?," "Will my SPIs [Student Perception of Instruction evaluation] influence this review process?", "Will students start taking online classes at another school because they are marked as Quality?"). Once those were acknowledged and addressed, the draft of QORC items was distributed for the instructors to review. It was interesting to note that the general consensus was, "Oh, this isn't so bad." They were also given the chance to sign up to participate in the course review process, as beta testers of sorts. The Quality Initiative manager continued to garner support and feedback from faculty for the QOCR process by presenting at high profile University events as well as the CDL Faculty Advisory Board. Members of CDL executive leadership are also sharing the message by visiting deans and chairs to garner higher level department support.

As is the case with any professional development, providing incentives is important to getting instructors involved. Currently, we do not offer formal incentives like stipends or course releases. However, we do offer items that can be valued, such as a congratulatory letter that is suitable for dossiers, attractive badges which can be placed within the online course for students to see, and a mention that the course will be recognized as "Quality"

within the state's online course catalog. Anecdotally, we have heard of people interested in participating because they seek the "competitive edge" in bolstering student enrollments.

INSTRUCTIONAL DESIGNERS AND OTHER SUPPORT STAFF

While communication with instructors is crucial, implementation of the review process will not be successful without "buy-in" from the instructional designers and other support staff (Table 2). At UCF, we have nearly 20 instructional designers, and 60 additional support staff who could potentially aid in the review process (course development, graphics, etc.).

Questions the task force first encountered from support staff were not unexpected. Instructional designers were concerned with the time commitment it would take to participate in the review process, when their plates were already full. Concerns about expectations also arose; how many reviews were expected to be completed each semester? How many instructors with which to engage? Are there consequences if the goals are not reached?

To address some of the initial concerns, overall framing of the process was necessary. It was emphasized that we have been engaging in course reviews to some degree through our interactions with faculty already. Formalizing a review process

Table 1. Communication Plan for Instructors: Key Message Points

Recommendations: Instructors
• Give instructors a chance to give input and voice concerns.
• Give instructors a chance to offer their online courses as beta testers.
• Identify possible "champions" for the quality cause.
• Create brief sheet of "message points" to share with interested instructors, which make it easy for them to say yes.
• Emphasize course design, rather than teaching.
• Identify the benefits the instructor will experience by participating in the review.
• Emphasize collaborative nature of the review process between instructor and ID—do *with*, not do *to*.

Table 2. Communication Plan for Support Staff: Key Message Points

Recommendations for Instructional Designers and Other Support Staff
• Let team voice concerns.
• Develop a series of team goals.
• Emphasize that the goal is simply to serve as a baseline and will help set expectations for the following semesters.
• Pair instructional designers up to support each other.
• Seek leadership to support the goals and fund incentives.
• Provide strategies to aid the process (recruitment strategies, customized emails, workflows).
• Personally meet with other teams and leads to support the effort.

makes it more systematic, and gives us a common ground/language/framework in which to work. It also gives us additional points for entry in building relationships with faculty, which is a core function of the instructional designer role at UCF. In addition, a series of team goals was set rather than an individual goal, with the intention of promoting cooperation and camaraderie. In addition, each ID was paired with one member of the task force, to gain further support. For the first semester implemented, the team goal was set to average one review per instructional designer, with a "stretch goal" of two reviews. Once reaching the stretch goal, an incentive will be offered (celebratory social event), funded by leadership.

Finally, training was provided in a step-by-step manner, putting the ID in the center of the process; "I'm an ID and about to embark on the course review process. What do I do first?" Several training sessions were provided in order to ensure all IDs could attend. The Quality Initiative manager also met with other coordinating teams to ensure that the purpose of the course reviews was understood.

CONCLUSION

There is no doubt that quality in an online course is the primary concern of all the players involved from students to administration. As the implementation of the qual-ity initiative moves forward, the challenges of policy formation and revision will play a major role in the improvement of the quality course designations at UCF. The key to the implementation is malleability and engagement on all levels as the adoption process plays out. If quality can be defined in quantitative deliverables with the correct branding, the attraction will be there for students as well as faculty to reach that badging standard. Communicating and implementing a quality course review process has the propensity to strengthen the quality of learning across the university, in both online and brick and mortar courses. Moreover, the brand and reputation of a university relies on the quality of learning, assured by a quality course review system.

This article provides the basic blueprint of implementing a course review process. We share the recommendations and lesson learned so far with others who are interested in similar opportunities. Future goals include introducing a course review process that would build on the current QOCR by focusing on "high quality" standards. Other important work includes ensuring alignment of the course review processes with local and state awards and professional development. Going beyond singular course review, we would also like to explore approaching an entire online program course review, in which all of the online courses within the program would be involved.

Student Satisfaction Rates

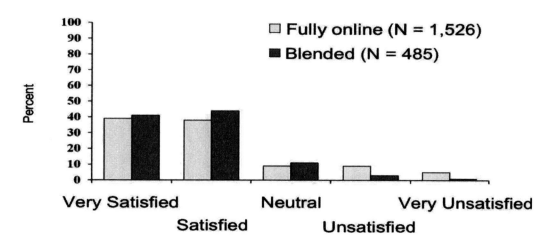

Faculty Satisfaction Rates

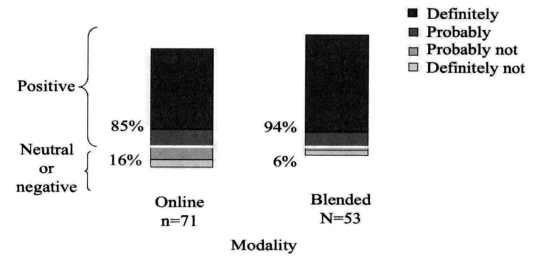

Source: Dziuban and Moskal (2016).

Student Success (A, B, or C grade)

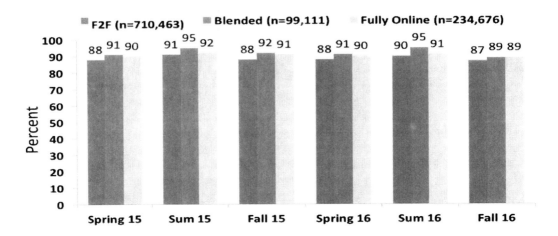

Student Withdrawal

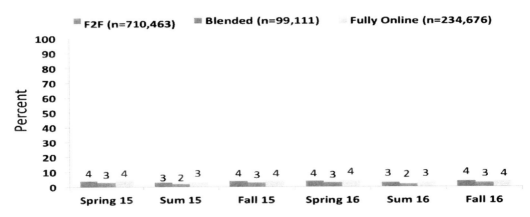

Source: Dziuban and Moskal (2017).

Appendix C: Quality Online Course Review Items

Section 1: Course Overview and Introduction

The course provides a clear starting point for students to begin accessing vital course components, such as syllabus, course schedule, course content, and assignments.

- The syllabus includes the following provost-required course information:
  - Course title and number;
  - Credit hours;
  - Course modality (W/M);
  - Name(s) of instructor(s);
  - Methods of contact (e.g., email address, phone number);
  - Office location;
  - Office hours (face-to-face or online);
  - Course description and purpose;
  - Course objectives and/or goals suited to level of course;
  - Course objectives and/or goals are measurable and clearly stated from learners' perspective;
  - Required and optional texts/course materials;
  - Grading policies (point/percentage breakdown of assignments, grading scale); and
  - Exam makeup policy.
- Information about academic integrity/honesty (UCF Golden Rule), campus policies, and FERPA are provided.
- Up-to-date information for students with disabilities to connect with UCF's Office of Student Accessibility Services (formerly Student Disability Services) is provided.
- General technical support information is provided for students and how to obtain (e.g., Webcourses@UCF Support contact information, Service Desk contact information).
- Online etiquette ("netiquette") expectations for course communication are clearly stated (e.g., discussion boards, email, chat, web conference).
- Expectations for instructor response time and feedback are clearly stated (e.g., questions, email, assignment feedback).
- Students are offered the opportunity to meet the instructor (e.g., introduction video, written instructor bio).
- The course has an explicit pace (e.g., a schedule) to which the students are introduced.

Section 2: Course Content

- The course has an explicit structure (e.g., organized in modules, units, and/or topics; tools not pertinent to the course are hidden in the menu) with a logical efficient navigation system throughout.
- The course offers a variety of instructional materials and media (e.g., external readings, assignments, discussions, videos) aligned with learning objectives and/or goals.
- Content is displayed in ways that support learning (e.g., chunking, Pages as opposed to Word docs and PDFs, etc.).
- The course offers opportunities for students to engage with the content, stating connection to learning activities or assessments, to enhance learning.
- Technical support information (e.g. tutorials, instructions) for using technology tools are provided.

Section 3: Assessment and Interaction

- Module objectives and/or goals are measurable, clearly stated from the learner's perspective, and aligned with course objectives and/or goals.
- Module objectives and/or goals are aligned with learning activities and assessments.
- Grading criteria for each learning activity is described (e.g. rubrics).

- Multiple methods and opportunities for students to demonstrate learning are offered.
- Technology tools support learning objectives and/or goals.
- Technology tools support a variety of interactions (e.g., student-to-student, student-to-content, student-to-instructor).
- The course offers opportunities for students to interact with other students to enhance learning (e.g., discussions, group work).
- The course offers opportunities for students to interact with the instructor to enhance learning (related to moderation/facilitation aspect).

REFERENCES

Baldwin, S., Ching, Y., & Hsu, Y. (2017). Online course design in higher education: A review of national and statewide evaluation instruments. *TechTrends*. doi:10.1007/s11528-017-0215-z

Bowser, A., Davis, K., Singleton, J., & Small, T. (2017). Professional learning: A collaborative model for online teaching and development. *SRATE Journal, 26*(1), 1–8.

Clinefelter, D. L., & Aslanian, C. B. (2017). *Online college students 2017: Comprehensive data on demands and preferences.* Louisville, KY: Learning. Retrieved from https://www .learninghouse.com/wp-content/uploads/2017/10/OCS-2017-Report.pdf

Crews, T. B., Bordonada, T. M., & Wilkinson, K. (2017). Student feedback on Quality Matters standards for online course design. *EDUCAUSE Review.* Retrieved from https://er .educause.edu/articles/2017/6/student-feedback-on-quality-matters-standards-for-online-course-design

Dziuban, C., & Moskal, P. (2016). *Distributed learning impact evaluation* [PowerPoint slides]. Retrieved from https://cdl.ucf.edu/research/dl-impact-evaluation/

Dziuban, C., & Moskal, P. (2017). *Center for Distributed Learning* [PowerPoint slides]. Retrieved from https://cdl.ucf.edu/research/dl-impact-evaluation/

Lee, J., & Dziuban, C. (2002). Using quality assurance strategies for online programs. *Educational Technology Review* [Online serial], *10*(2), 69–78.

Lenert, K. A., & Janes, D. P. (2017). The incorporation of quality attributes into online course design in higher education. *International Journal of E-Learning and Distance Education, 32*(1). Retrieved from http://www.ijede.ca/index.php/jde/article/view/987/1660

MarylandOnline, Inc. (2017a). *About QM.* Retrieved from the Quality Matters website: https://www.qualitymatters.org/why-quality-matters/about-qm

MarylandOnline, Inc. (2017b). *QM impact summary.* Retrieved from the Quality Matters website: https://www.qualitymatters.org/qa-resources/resource-center/articles-resources/qm-impact-summary

Mitchell, R. G. (2010). Approaching common ground: Defining quality in online education. *New Directions For Community Colleges,* (150), 89–94.

Thompson, K. (2008, June 7). What is online course quality? [Web log post]. Retrieved from http://ofcoursesonline.com/?p=122

Truman, B., Futch, L., Thompson, K., & Yonekura, F. (1999). *UCF's support for teaching and learning online: CD-ROM development, faculty development, and statewide training.* Retrieved from https://www.educause.edu/ir/library/html/edu9906/edu9906.html

Facilitating Interactive Relationships With Students Online

Recommendations From Counselor Educators

Kristin A. Vincenzes and Meredith Drew

MOTIVATING THE FACELESS STUDENT

In 2012, there were over 21,147,055 students who were distance learners (National Center for Educational Statistics, 2015). Due to the astonishing trend in online learning, higher education is branching out and developing blended and fully online programs. Currently the Council for Accreditation of Counseling and Related Educational Programs (CACREP) has 752 programs that are accredited (CACREP, 2015). Of those programs, 24 programs are online (CACREP, 2015). As more and more counseling programs are integrating the online learning format, it is essential for counselor educators to understand the unique benefits and challenges to teaching online. Furthermore, counselor educators need to develop a new approach to establishing positive learning communities, which will inevitably help motivate the online learners to be

Kristin A. Vincenzes,
Social Work and Clinical Mental Health
Counseling, Lock Haven University,
401 N. Fairview Street, Akeley 117,
Lock Haven, PA 17745.
E-mail: KAV813@lockhaven.edu

Meredith Drew,
Special Education and Counseling,
William Paterson University at Wayne,
1600 Valley Road, Room 3005,
Wayne, NJ, 07470.
E-mail: drewm2@wpunj.edu

successful with both their education as well as the counseling profession.

ONLINE LEARNING

Garrison and Kanuka (2004) believe that online learning occurs on a continuum depending on the amount of technological integration that occurs within the course. For example, one end of the online learning has very minimal technological integration, the middle of the continuum offers a delicate "blending" of technology and classroom strategies, while the opposite side of the spectrum is fully online learning (Garrison & Kanuka, 2004). For programs that wish to be fully online and require no face-to-face component, there are various benefits and challenges to analyze.

BENEFITS TO ONLINE PROGRAMS

Higher education institutions are particularly interested in distance education programs because they often result in large financial returns (Appana, 2008). By offering online programs, it reduces the cost to universities. For example, they reduce the pressure of resources to be at a physical location (Bowen, Chingos, Lack, & Nygren, 2013). With various resources and information at one's fingertips via the Web and online databases, students can access research without the university needing to have on-site libraries and research centers. In addition, online learning aids in the reduction of overhead costs for running facilities, which include: building maintenance, utility costs, and additional hired personnel for grounds upkeep (Smart & Cappel, 2006). Finally, colleges and universities do not need to worry about the overuse of facilities or managing where classes will take place each semester (Bartley & Golek, 2004).

Online learning is not only beneficial to the institution as a whole, but it offers students many benefits as well. Shea, Stone, and Delahunty (2015) discussed that this modality of learning eases many burdens of current learners. For example, students do not have the cost of traveling to the school, particularly if there's not a school near the current location of the student. The flexibility that online learning offers is also important because students have more freedom to choose the time, place, and pace of their studies (Ryan, 2001).

Online learning promotes multicultural learning opportunities amongst the student body by attracting, enrolling, and retaining a diverse group of students (CACREP, 2016, 1.K). By offering online programs, students may attend from all over the world. This enhances the academic unit, especially those that are CACREP accredited, by encouraging students to learn multicultural and pluralistic characteristics, heritages, attitudes, beliefs, understandings, and acculturative experiences by engaging with their national and international peers (CACREP, 2016, F.2.a & F.2.d). In addition, online learning helps students to maintain the multiple roles and obligations they have outside of being a student (Fairchild, 2003). This is important for those students who are working, have families, and or other personal/professional commitments. Since many of the online students have multiple roles in their lives, it brings a unique type of student to the classroom, thus drawing on professional level peers (Holzweiss, Joyner, Fuller, Henderson, & Young, 2014). These students increase the critical analysis, developmental thinking, and broaden the application of the learning process for the entire class. Furthermore, the characteristics of online learners tend to have high standards for themselves, while also maintaining skills such as good time management, self-motivation, and discipline (Serwatka, 2003).

CHALLENGES WITH ONLINE PROGRAMS

While online learning has many benefits, there are also challenges. One common issue for many online programs is the retention rates. There tends to be a higher frequency of dropouts, which can be between 30%–50% (Allen & Seaman, 2010). The most common factors that impact the dropout rates include: problems negotiating technology and struggling with navigating course content (Tyler-Smith, 2006). Students may not clearly understand course standards or the course delivery system (Ali, Ramay, & Shahzad, 2011), which can be further impacted by the amount of support and/or computer literacy that the student has with technology (Furlonger & Genic, 2014). Technology issues, such as poor connections, sounds, visuals, and overloaded networks also impact the student's satisfaction with online learning (Appana, 2008).

Fortunately, research indicates that programs can increase the rates of student satisfaction and reduce dropout rates with various interventions. For example, research found that by encouraging early and ongoing interaction with the faculty, it increased factors leading to student satisfaction (Horzum, 2015; Shea, Stone, & Delahunty, 2015). Furthermore, Horzum (2015) found that students expressed a desire for more interactive tools, increased social presence, and encouragement of active participation. These strategies could be coupled with Appana's (2008) recommendations of offering special technological training, providing ongoing support, and keeping a good rapport regarding the technology between staff and students. All of these combined interventions could significantly impact the students' satisfaction, thus potentially increasing the success of the program.

ONLINE LEARNING IN COUNSELOR EDUCATION PROGRAMS

After understanding the strengths and challenges of online learning in general, it's important to discuss the vitality of it, particularly as it applies to counselor edu-

cation programs. Distance programs offer the unique ability to diversify the student body and faculty who teach in the program. By offering online counselor education programs, "systematic efforts [can be used] to attract, enroll, and retain a diverse group of students and to create and support an inclusive learning community" (CACREP, 2016, 1.K). These same efforts can be infused to employ a diverse faculty (CACREP, 2016, 1.Q) to enhance the counselor education team. With diverse faculty, the students will learn a multitude of teaching and therapeutic styles. In turn, these experiences will enhance the students' capability to work with a diverse clientele.

A second influential strength for online counselor education programs focuses on the learning opportunities between peers. By increasing the prospect of multiculturalism within the program, it enhances the quality of the program. For example, online learning increases the potential for international students to enroll due to the ability to have access to the learning format from anywhere in the world (Katz & Associates, 1999). With international students, classes can expand learning opportunities for cultural diversity to include discussions on diverse spiritual beliefs and how that might impact the clients' and counselors' worldviews (CACREP, 2016, F.2.g). Furthermore, because online programs allow for demographically diverse students to attend, students can learn the impacts of heritage, attitudes, beliefs, understandings, and acculturative experiences from each other (CACREP, 2016, F.2.d). Discussions on the effects of power and privilege as well as help-seeking behaviors of diverse individuals (CACREP, 2016, F.2.e and f) can occur more fluidly when the student body is composed of various multicultural backgrounds and experiences. Finally, student diversity within a counselor education program may create a unique environment for peers to supportively challenge one another to identify and eliminate barriers, prejudices, and processes of intentional and unintentional oppression and discrimination (CACREP, 2016, F.2.h).

While online programs can attract a very diverse group of students, there are noteworthy challenges, particularly for programs that are training mental health counselors. For example, many people fear that online learning can create a relational disconnect between students and faculty because counseling at its core focuses on the ability to build relationships. How can counselor educators do this through the use of technology? As one counselor educator wrote about his journey from teaching face to face to teaching online, "Online education appeared, from the outside, to be nothing more than input and output, treating students as they, themselves were computers" (Dietrich, 2015, p. 93). Freeman and Tremblay (2013) found that online instructors actually felt disconnected from their students, which boiled down to a perception of not truly knowing their students.

In counselor education programs, the ability to maintain and sustain relationships with our students is pivotal. This relationship can create a parallel processing in which we model skills for building and fostering a therapeutic working relationship. Unfortunately, this task of a counselor educator can be inhibited due to technological barriers when education occurs online. Cicco (2013) recommended that when creating an online counseling skills course, there needs to be various opportunities for students and faculty to communicate. This may be via 1-hour webinars or synchronous methods to improve communication and relationships between peers and faculty or, as Andrade (2008) recommended, campus advisement meetings, attending off-campus professional development events, or conferences.

Carl Rogers discussed the importance of establishing a therapeutic alliance by exemplifying genuine unconditional positive regard and empathy. These particular concepts may be easy to read in a textbook; however, understanding what it looks like, sounds like, and feels like can be difficult to show in an online learning format because it lacks the contact and nonverbal cues that face-to-face interaction can offer (Appana, 2008). The lack of face-to-face interactions can impact the ability for counselor educators to further demonstrate professional identity and counseling skills. Finally, online programs may inhibit the collaborative approach between students, their peers, and the instructor, which has been found to be effective in fostering the learning process (Horzum, 2015).

PURPOSE

Research shows that learning communities and establishing a relationship with students correlates with an increase in both academic success and retention rates. In traditional brick-and-mortar institutions, class time, office hours, and student meetings help to achieve this relationship; however, when programs are offered via online learning environments, establishing this relationship can pose a significant challenge. From the humanistic approach of counselor education and the belief that fostering and modeling positive working relationships is a pivotal strategy to developing competent future counselors, the current study examined the participants' belief about the importance of relationships in helping online students to be successful. Furthermore, the study examined effective strategies that current counselor educators are using to help establish relationships and actively engage with their students.

RESEARCH DESIGN

A quantitative survey research design was chosen for this study. In order to gain knowledge about new strategies and ideas used to facilitate relationships and model counselor professional identity, the research used a structured open-ended questionnaire that was facilitated through the use of an online survey via Survey Monkey (see Appendix A). Counselor educators currently in the field received the surveys so that the researchers could understand the experiences and ideas shared by counselor educators.

DATA COLLECTION

This quantitative study used volunteer purposive sampling to identify current counselor educators in brick-and-mortar, blended, and fully online academic programs. The only inclusion criterion was that the participants needed to teach at least one course online in a counselor education program. A solicitation e-mail went out to counselor educators, cesnet.com listserv, as well as program directors from different online counseling programs. They were also asked to forward the advertisement to any colleagues who teach online.

Once the participants received the e-mail advertisement, they decided if they wanted to participate. If they wanted to volunteer, the participants clicked on a link at the bottom of the advertisement. The link automatically directed them to an informed consent to read. Participants provided their consent by clicking on the link on the bottom of the informed consent. Then they completed a short background questionnaire followed by questions pertaining to strategies the online educator uses to connect and build relationships with their students.

DATA ANALYSIS

The survey gathered demographic information and asked open-ended questions to facilitate a more comprehensive opportunity to understand the experiences of counselor educators. Through the collection of answers, the data were organized into categories and themes that illustrated

the views of counselor educators in the field. These themes were created by using exact matches in NVivo. Exact matches identified words (including synonyms) that were repeated throughout the participants' responses. Based on the identified themes, the researchers interpreted the information to more thoroughly understand the uniqueness of online education and influential strategies that may be beneficial to facilitating positive working relationships with students.

RESULTS

Of the 36 participants (14 males and 22 females) who responded and completed the survey, 34 were counselor educators and 34 participants taught online. Participants ranged from 27 to 59 years of age. The ethnicity of the participants were: 31 Caucasian, 2 Hispanic, 1 Asian American, 1 African American, and 1 chose not to answer. The average number of years the participants taught was 8.62.

The survey included a variety of open-ended questions. The first question asked about the importance of relationships. Specifically: How does the relationship between the counselor educator and counseling students affect the development of counselor identity in the student? Some of the responses received were:

- "It is important and can model either successful or unsuccessful ways to be a counselor depending on the skill level and the professional identity of the Counselor Educator."
- "Wow, not sure I can summarize it briefly. It's essential. We are models, gatekeepers, nurturers for the next generation of counselors. Modeling of good communication with students and high levels of feedback do translate, I believe into similar skills the student is developing related to counselor effectiveness."
- "This is my primary concern with online learning in our field. Students learn

how to write, and how to answer questions, but they do not learn to engage with others in the moment."

- "Our students look up to us and hope to emulate us. I am an MFT, so I believe strongly in isomorphism. To make effective counselors, we have to first look in the mirror. It's OUR job to connect with students, the same way it is our job to connect with clients. We have the power in the relationship, so we must be the ones who reach out to students. This really doesn't change between online teaching and f2f teaching."
- "Counselor Educators are role models for our students. The skills we demonstrate as we teach will influence their skills and performance. If we reflect the counseling skills we hope to see in our students, we will encourage them to emulate these skills with their clients and continue to work toward developing themselves professionally."
- "It makes a tremendous difference, counseling students and counselor educators that build relationships during the program end up engaging in professional activities outside the program—presentations, working together on projects, providing references for positions, etc. The counselor identity is strong when the counselor educators model this identity and are engaging with students even beyond the classroom for real life application of what we teach."
- "Absolutely! When you have a relationship and they respect you, the students are more likely to want to emulate you. I tell my students about professional activities I am involved in. I encourage them to join me."

A follow-up question looked at the strategies counselor educators use to build relationships with online students. The categorical themes included: connection ($N = 20$), presence ($N = 19$), accessibility ($N = 17$), responsiveness ($N = 17$), and delivery ($N = 10$). With regards to connection, participants stated the importance of getting to know the students as people as well as students (to include introduction discussions/identity collage and informal discussion areas where both students and the professor provide personal and professional introductions). The theme of connection also encapsulated the educators' "passion" and "enthusiasm" for the profession. Participants stated the importance of online educators encouraging connection between peers outside of the classroom experience. Finally, participants discussed the need for online educators to recognize students who are struggling and to actively reach out to them.

The next two themes focused on "presence" and "accessibility." "Presence" referred to the educator's commitment to be active in the course. For example, how often does the instructor check-in with the students or respond to discussions occurring in the course. How does the instructor connect with the students and build those relationships? In the research, the theme of "presence" included statements about consistent involvement in online discussions (especially at the beginning of the course). It was also mentioned that the use of regular "News Announcements," "Mainframes," "Welcoming Emails," and "Inspirational Quotes" are beneficial to establishing relationships. The parallel theme of "accessibility" was clearly stated by the ease of access to the professor to include cell phone, e-mail, Skype, and synchronous opportunities. Essentially, if the student had a question, needed to practice a skill, or had any difficulty with a concept, how easily and comfortably could a student reach out to his or her instructor.

With regards to "responsiveness," online educators stated the importance of quick feedback that was specific, detailed, and personal to each individual student. Participants commented about the importance of valuing the quality of work over the due dates. When providing feedback, participants mentioned the value of offering more praise than criticism and validating the students' perspectives/questions. Finally, educators mentioned the need to focus on participation in discussion board's verses content and APA.

The last theme involved the delivery methods the educator used to help establish relationships. For example, participants stated the value of using various modes of technology. Furthermore, participants discussed the importance of integrating structured online delivery to include: clear expectations, employing social constructivist approaches, integrating audio/video lectures/format /virtual class, using peer evaluation, and increasing the use challenging assignments as the semester continues.

LIMITATIONS

This study has a few limitations. The first limitation relates to the external reliability and generalizability of the results. Since the sample size was rather small at only 34 participants, the data collected may not be generalizable to the larger population of online counselor educators. While the current sample implied a commitment from the counselor educator to be willing to provide opportunities for students to interact in a meaningful way, not all counselor educators may feel the same way. Due to the small sample size, it cannot be assumed that all counselor educators will value the importance of interacting with students and creating working relationships.

The small sample size may also impact the credibility of the results in the eyes of administrators. While many participants discussed the importance of integrating multiple technological modalities, college and university administrators may not value these results due to the sample size. This could impact the administrations' unwillingness to purchase various technologies to advance the connection between students and faculty.

Another limitation of the current study relates to the potential biases of the researchers. When analyzing the data and creating themes, qualitative analysis requires the introspection of the researcher. With this in mind, the themes discovered could have been influenced by the personal values of the researchers. This limitation could further impact both the internal and external reliability of the study.

A final limitation refers to the internal validity of the results. First, the participants' answers may have been skewed due to the position of the researchers. For example, the participants may have answered the questions by discussing what they feel they "should" do as a counselor educator rather than what they truly do. This could have occurred because participants were informed that the researchers themselves were counselor educators. Furthermore, it could be that since the researchers did not observe the participants in their natural teacher setting, the answers provided to each question may not replicate the actual strategies used.

DISCUSSION

Hrastinski (2009) discussed the need for online education to go beyond simply talking and writing. Many online programs rely on the writing component through discussion boards, papers, and other forms of written assignments. Some programs are now integrating synchronous components such as Blackboard Collaborate, Google Hangouts, or Digital Samba. These synchronous modalities allow for faculty and students to communicate in real time, which is a great resource to increase the connection with each other; however, educators need to do even more to create successful students and thus a successful program.

The information collected from the participants in the current study collaborated prior research that pointed to the importance of connection and presence. When counselor educators can connect with their students through a positive online presence, it is possible to promote learning communities where students can feel supported by their peers and faculty members (Glassmeyer, Dibbs, & Thomas Jensen, 2011). Hudson, Hudson, and Steel (2006) found that a student's sense of belonging correlated to their success in the program. By establishing relationships with our students and thus creating supportive learning communities, students may be able to be more successful in online programs.

Supportive learning environments and faculty interactions also has been found to impact attrition rates for online programs. Attrition rates are found to be 10%–20% higher for online programs (Angelino, Williams, & Natvig, 2007) thus impacting the stability of a program. Schaffhauser (2009) reported multiple reasons for the astonishing attrition rate for online programs, including: financial challenges (41%), life events (32%), health issues (23%), lack of motivation (21%), and lack of faculty interaction (21%). It is proposed that by establishing relationships with online students through connection, presence, and accessibility (all three themes that were found in the current research) that counselor educators may be able to increase the motivation within the students. This motivation combined with the positive faculty interactions may sustain more online programs.

Finally, relationships between educators and students may also be an influential component of modeling the counselor identity for the faceless student. Through the interactions that counselor educators have with their students, it is possible for students to observe the essential qualities of a counseling professional. Albert Bandura (1986) discussed the influential vitality of modeling for people to learn. If counselor educators can establish relationships with online students through connection, presence, and accessibility, they can model the counselor's role in establish-ing rapport and a working relationship with his/her client.

CONCLUSION

The *Chronicle of Higher Education* (Chronicle Research Services, 2009) projected that by 2020 over 60% of individuals will be taking all of their courses online. As online education programs continue to grow in both interest as well as necessity, it is proposed that there will also be an influx of counselor education programs to be offered solely online. That National Center for Education Statistics (2015) also found an increase with individuals going for a master's degree or higher, stating the increase rose from 5% in 1995 to 8% in 2014. While 3% may not seem like a lot, interest is rising. With these statistics, counselor educators need to wholeheartedly reflect on how to establish relationships with their students via online modalities so that online programs, as well as the enrolled students, can be successful.

APPENDIX A

Please answer the following questions.

1. Gender (male, female, other)
2. Age (actual age in years)
3. Ethnicity (non-Hispanic White, Hispanic, American Indian/Alaska Native, Asian American, Pacific Islander, African American, other, prefer not to answer)
4. Do you teach online? (yes or no)
5. If yes, is your program blended, online-only, other-please specify)
6. How many students are enrolled in your academic program? (0–50, 51–100, 101–150, 151– +)
7. How many students, on average, are in one of your online courses? (5–10, 11–15, 16–20, 21–25, 26–30, 31 and higher)
8. Where is your institution located? (Western Region, Eastern Region, Mid-

west, Southern, Northern, International—Please specify which country)

9. Do you teach undergraduate, graduate, or both? (undergraduate, graduate, or both)

10. How long have you been teaching? (in years)

11. Are you a counselor educator? (yes or no)

   o Yes … How long have you been a counselor educator? (in years)

   o No … What area of study do you teach in? (business/management, communications, criminal justice/history/ political science, education, information technology, nursing/health sciences, human services/social work, other: _____)

12. Please rate the following statements (1-no value, 2-minimal value, 3-value, 4-great value) while reflecting on your work as an online educator.

   o The relationship between teacher and student is crucial to a students' academic success.

   o The counselor educator's role in promoting the relationship between educator and students.

   o The student's willingness to participate in building a relationship between that student and the educator.

   o Availability of the student

   o Availability of the educator

   o Ease of accessibility (i.e. mobile phone, e-mail, text, etc.)

   o Approachability of the student

   o Approachability of the Educator

   o The use multiple media sources (i.e. online chats, Skype, telephone, e-mail, text) to support the development of student relationships.

13. What strategies do you use to develop your relationship with students?

14. What strategies have you tried that were not successful?

15. What are you most successful with in creating your student relationships?

16. What challenges present as a result of the online format that are distinct from the challenges that might otherwise present in a bricks-and-mortar program?

17. How does the relationship between the counselor educator and counseling students affect the development of counselor identity in the student?

REFERENCES

Ali, A., Ramay, M. I., & Shahzad, M. (2011). Key factors in distance learning sources: A study of Allama Iqbal Open University (AIOU) Islamabad, Pakistan. *Turkish Online Journal of Distance Education, 12*(2), 114–127.

Allen, I. E., & Seaman, J. (2010). *Learning on demand: Online education in the United States.* Retrieved from http://sloansonsortium.org/publications/survey/pdf/learbingondemand.pdf

Andrade, H. (2008). Self-assessment through rubrics. *Educational Leadership, 65*(4), 60–63.

Angelino, L. M., Williams, F. K., & Natvig, D. (2007). Strategies to engage online students and reduce attrition rates. *The Journal of Educators Online, 4*(2), 1–14. Retrieved from www.thejeo.com/Volume4Number2/Angelino%20Final.pdf

Appana, S. (2008). A review of benefits and limitations of online learning in the context of the student, the instructor, and the tenured faculty. *International Journal on E-learning, 7*(1), 5–22.

Banathy, B. (1994). Designing educational systems: Creating our future in a changing world. In C. M. Reigeluth & R. J. Garfinkle (Eds.), *Systematic change in education* (pp. 27–34). Englewood Cliffs, NJ: Educational Technology.

Bandura, A. (1986). *Social foundations of thought and action: A social cognitive theory.* Englewood Cliffs, NJ: Prentice-Hall.

Bartley, Z., & Golek, J. H. (2004). Evaluating the cost effectiveness of online and face-to-face instruction. *Educational Technology and Society, 7*(4), 167–175.

Bowen, W. G., Chingos, M. M., Lack, K. A., & Nygren, T. I. (2014). Interactive learning online at public universities: Evidence from a six-campus randomized trial. *Journal of Policy Analysis and Management, 33*(1), 94–111.

Chronicle Research Services. (2009). *The college of 2020: Students.* Retrieved from https://www.acui.org/uploadedFiles/_PUBLISHED_CONTENT/Programs/Professional_Development/2011_Events/Chronicle%20Article%202020%20Students.pdf

Council for the Accreditation of Counseling & Related Educational Programs. (2016). 2016 CACREP Standards. Retrieved from http://www.cacrep.org/forprograms/2016-cacrep-standards/

Dietrich, D. C. (2015). Observations of a reluctant online instructor: Transitioning from the classroom to the computer. *College Teaching, 63*(3), 93–98.

Fairchild, E. E. (2003). Multiple roles of adult learners. *New Directions for Student Services, 102,* 111–116.

Freeman, W., & Tremblay, T. (2013). Design considerations for supporting reluctant adoption of blended learning. *Journal of Online Learning and Teaching, 9*(1), 80–88.

Furlonger, B., & Genic, E. (2014). Comparing satisfaction, life-stress, coping, and academic performance of counseling students in on-campus and distance education learning environments. *Australian Journal of Guidance and Counseling, 24*(1), 76–89. doi: 10.1017/jgc.2014.2

Garrison, D. R., & Kanuka, H. (2004). Blended learning: Uncovering its transformative potential in higher education. *The Internet and Higher Education, 7*(2), 95–105.

Glassmeyer, D. M., Dibbs, R. A., & Thomas Jensen, R. (2011). Determining utility of formative assessment through virtual community: Perspectives of online graduate students. *Quarterly Review of Distance Education, 12*(1), 23–35.

Holzweiss, P. C., Joyner, S. A., Fuller, M. B., Henderson, S., & Young, R. (2014). Online graduate students' perceptions of best learning experiences. *Distance Education, 35*(3), 311–323. doi:10.1080/01587919.2015.955262

Horzum, M. B. (2015). Interaction, structure, social presence, and satisfaction in online learning. *Eurasia Journal of Mathematics, Science, and Technology, 11*(3), 505–512. doi:10.12973/Eurasia.2014.1324a

Hrastinski, S. (2009). A theory of online learning as online participation. *Computers & Education, 52*(1), 78–82.

Hudson, B., Hudson, A., & Steel, J. (2006). Orchestrating interdependence in an international online learning community. *British Journal of Educational Technology, 37*(5), 733–748. doi.org/10.111/j.1467-8535.2006.00552.x

Katz, R., & Associates. (1999). *Dancing with the devil: Information technology and the new competition in higher education.* San Francisco, CA: Jossey Bass.

National Center for Educational Statistics (2015). *Fast facts: Educational attainment.* Retrieved from https://nces.ed.gov/fastfacts/display.asp?id=27

Ryan, S. (2001). Is online learning right for you? *American Agent & Broker, 73*(6), 54–58.

Schaffhauser, D. (2009). *Survey reports many online learners never seek help before dropping out.* Retrieved from http://www.campustechnology.com/Articles/2009/01/09/Survey-Reports-Many-Online-Learners-Never-Seek-Help-Before-Dropping-Out.aspx

Serwatka, J. (2003). Assessment in online CIS courses. *Journal of Computer Information Systems, 43*(3), 16–20.

Shea, S. O., Stone, C., & Delahunty, J. (2015). "I feel like I am at university even though I am online." Exploring how students narrate their engagement with higher education institutions in an online learning environment. *Distance Education, 36*(6), 41–58. doi:10.1080/01587919.2015.1019970

Smart, K. L., & Cappel, J. J. (2006). Students' perceptions of online learning: A comparative study. *Journal of Information Technology Education, 5,* 201–214.

Tyler-Smith, K. (2006). Early attrition among first time e-learners: A review of factors that contribute to drop-out, withdrawal, and non-completion rates of adult learners undertaking e-learning programmes. *Journal of Online Learning & Teaching, 2*(2), 73–85.

Psychomotor Skills, Physical Therapy, and a Hybrid Course

A Case Study

Melissa J. Lazinski

INTRODUCTION

Approximately 75% of the content of a typical doctor of physical therapy (PT) course does not require the instructor and students to be together in the same classroom, laboratory, or clinic. Physical therapist education includes a large amount of psychomotor clinical skills. Traditionally, psychomotor skills are taught face to face in laboratory courses with teacher-led skill

Melissa Lazinski,
Associate Professor, Physical Therapy,
Dr. Pallavi Patel College of Health Care
Sciences, Nova Southeastern University.
Telephone: (813) 574-5313.
E-mail: mj.lazinski@nova.edu

introduction and demonstration followed by student practice with instructor feedback (Gaida et al., 2016; Maloney, Storr, Paynter, Morgan, & Ilic, 2013). A goal of hybrid course redesign is to balance elements essential to face to face with those that can be delivered online. Ideally, online and face-to-face classrooms work in a symbiotic way without being duplicative. The dynamic nature of learning psychomotor skills makes hybrid redesign of PT courses challenging. This article describes the redesign of a traditional PT lab course using the community of inquiry (CoI) model as a framework and Google Blogger as the main platform for an online skills lab. A description and discussion of course design, time allocations, student learning outcomes, and student perceptions are provided.

Student needs for flexibility and rising health care workforce demands influence a trend toward hybrid delivery in health care education; however, substantiation of the ways technology can effectively replace face-to-face instruction is needed (Brandt, Quake-Rapp, Shanedling, Spannaus-Martin, & Martin, 2010). Hybrid education is a category of distance education in which online activities replace face-to-face activities. This contrasts with other models of blended learning such as a *flipped* classroom, which incorporate online instruction as an adjunct to face-to-face instruction without a reduction of face-to-face time. Garrison and Vaughn (2008) described hybrid or blended learning as a "thoughtful fusion of face-to-face and online learning experiences" (p. 8). The CoI model provides a framework for hybrid course design using online and face-to-face instruction in a way that each mode enhances without duplicating the other (Garrison, Anderson, & Archer, 2010). The mixture of online and face-to-face activities varies from case to case (Means et al., 2013). In the CoI model, three essential components overlap to create an educational experience: *teaching presence, cognitive presence*, and *social presence* (Garrison & Vaughn, 2008; see Figure 1). Teaching presence is the design of class activities, facilitation of discourse, and direction of instruction. Cognitive presence comes as students engage, explore, and integrate the course content. Social presence occurs as class participants interact in open communication, to build camaraderie and group cohesion (Garrison & Vaughn, 2008).

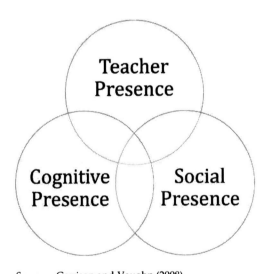

Source: Garrison and Vaughn (2008).

Figure 1. Community of inquiry model

EDUCATIONAL TECHNOLOGY IN PHYSICAL THERAPY EDUCATION

Recent systematic reviews found that integration of educational technologies in health care education was equivalent or better than traditional teaching methods alone (George et al., 2014; Rasmussen et al., 2014). Heterogeneity of studies prevents more definitive conclusions, but emerging evidence supports the use of educational technologies in PT education. A variety of approaches have been described including flipped classroom methods, using supplemental technology resources, and using collaborative technology tools. As in higher education in general, PT education most commonly uses technology to teach didactic content or achieve cognitive objectives (Rowe, Bozalek, & Frantz, 2013). In studies comparing a flipped model to traditional teaching methods for didactic content, student learning outcomes and perceptions varied, but variation in methods may account for some of the differences. One study found improved student learning outcomes using flipped methods (Boucher, Robertson, Wainner, & Sanders, 2013). Another found no difference in overall student performance scores, but those in the flipped group did better with higher order questions (Bayliss & Warden, 2011). A third found no difference in student achievement between traditional and flipped methods (Murray, McCallum, & Petrosino, 2014). In this case, students were provided previewing materials, but face-to-face class times began with 20-30 minute lectures, which may have undermined the need for preparation, an important component of the flipped model. Student perceptions were positive for previewing prerecorded lectures before class (Boucher et al., 2013), but showed no increased preference for previewing PowerPoint lecture slides (not recordings) (Bayliss & Warden, 2011). The variety of techniques used make it difficult to draw global conclusions.

Supplemental online or computer activities in addition to traditional instruction have shown favorable results in cognitive learning outcomes and student perceptions, in higher education in general (Cain & Pitre, 2008; Meyer, 2014). In a neurological PT course, it was found that students with access to supplemental computer modules with embedded video and practice questions had better clinical reasoning and learning outcomes compared to receiving traditional lecture and lab alone (Veneri & Gannotti, 2014). In addition, student perceptions of learning were better in the group with the added computer modules. Similarly, Gardner et al., (2016) investigated student perceptions of an e-learning package to teach PT students about rheumatoid arthritis. The e-learning package was given in addition to three live lectures about general chronic disease management. Students had positive perceptions of the experience and preferred a blended approach to the subject matter. Rowe and colleagues (2013) used Google Drive as a platform for a blended PT case activity and found that students valued the authentic learning approach and had shifts in their perceptions about learning. In an online PT pharmacology course that incorporated a collaborative learning activity, students had positive attitudes about the course design without a change in the grade distribution (Pittenger & Olson-Kellogg, 2012).

Teaching psychomotor skills with educational technologies and blended methods has emerging support in the literature, but like didactic content there are a variety of methods and outcomes reported. Some studies found no difference in outcomes between traditional and methods using technology (Maloney, Storr, Paynter, et al., 2013; VanDuijn, Swanick, & Donald, 2014), and others found improved outcomes with the use of technology (Arroyo-Morales et al., 2012; Maloney, Storr, Morgan, & Ilic, 2013; Preston et al., 2012). Physical therapy students have reported higher perceived satisfaction with blended methods of teaching psychomotor skills, particularly including video versus traditional methods (Coffee & Hillier, 2008; Gaida et al., 2016; Hurst, 2016; Maloney, Storr, Morgan, et al. 2013; Maloney, Storr, Paynter, et al., 2013). Video has been show to enhance engagement, social presence, and learning (Kliger & Pfeiffer, 2011). Further, incorporating student-produced skill demonstration videos (self-videos) were found to improve student skill performance on assessments and increase students' perceptions of educational value over traditional teaching methods (Maloney, Storr, Morgan, et al., 2013; Maloney, Storr, Paynter, et al., 2013).

Regardless of approach, mastering psychomotor skills requires instructor presence through feedback. Traditionally this occurs in the classroom setting face-to-face (Gaida et al., 2016); however, video can be used as a vehicle for receiving feedback at a distance. Student self-videos of skill performance have been effectively used to give formative feedback on performance at a distance (Maloney, Storr, Morgan, et al., 2013; Maloney, Storr, Paynter, et al., 2013).

Available studies investigating the use of blended models or supplemental education technologies in PT education have studied learning outcomes, student perceptions, and satisfaction with favorable findings. No study could be found that investigated changes in the distribution of time as an outcome. This is an important consideration in the implementation of a hybrid course design in which face-to-face time is replaced by online time, because the shift in time allocation has implications for students and faculty. In addition, heterogeneity of studied instructional methods makes findings difficult to interpret (George et al., 2014; Rasmussen et al., 2014; Veneri, 2011). Evidence is lacking for teaching psychomotor skills in a hybrid course whereby online instruction replaces traditional face-to-face instruction.

CASE DESCRIPTION

The course was a 1-credit hour laboratory course focused on psychomotor and affective objectives of performing surface palpation. It was part of the first-year curriculum of the Nova Southeastern University Hybrid Doctor of Physical Therapy Program (HDPT). The course was converted to hybrid from an existing traditional course that met weekly. The redesigned hybrid course occurred in a 16-week semester with four face-to-face on-campus institutes. Four-day on-campus institutes took place throughout the semester at the end of every fourth week (Thursday through Sunday). The class met for a 3-hour face-to-face lab session at each on-campus institute for a total of 12 face-to-face instructional hours. This equates to 25% of the face-to-face time if the course was taught traditionally (completely face to face), with the remainder of class-time (75%) occurring online.

Initial course redesign began by differentiating activities that must occur face-to-face from those that could occur online. The conclusion was that two key components must occur face to face: (a) face-to-face practice with feedback and (b) skills assessment. Given the on-campus institute time constraints, it was decided students should have an introduction and be practicing skills online in preparation for face-to-face time. The layout of the course schedule placed one body region in each week for 12 weeks, with 4 weeks remaining at the end of the course for review of cardinal plane joint motions and application of palpated landmarks to postural assessment.

The course design was constructed with components that created the elements of the CoI model (see Figure 2). Activities that supported these design components were carefully selected with the underlying pedagogy in mind and the understanding that technology does not drive student achievement (Means, Toyama, Murphy, Bakia, & Jones, 2010; Meyer, 2014).

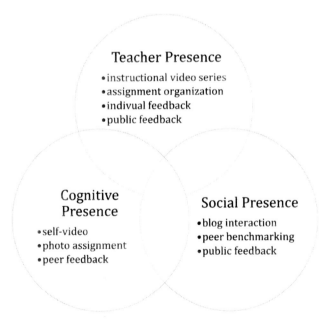

Teacher Presence
• instructional video series
• assignment organization
• indivual feedback
• public feedback

Cognitive Presence
• self-video
• photo assignment
• peer feedback

Social Presence
• blog interaction
• peer benchmarking
• public feedback

Figure 2. Community of inquiry model complete with course design components.

ONLINE CLASSROOM

Constrained face-to-face time required students to arrive to the physical classroom having been introduced to a skill set and having basic proficiency. To include instruction, deliberate practice, and feedback in a meaningful way during online time, instructor, cognitive, and social presence were considered in the online course design. Instructional content was delivered via textbook and video. A text was selected for its format, engaging illustrations, and accompanying instructional DVD. Supplemental videos were produced by the course instructor and published online for content not adequately covered by the text-companion DVD.

Deliberate practice and feedback were incorporated in course design through weekly online assignments with the goal of moving beyond skill introduction and toward proficiency prior to on-campus institute. To reach proficiency with psychomotor skills requires feedback. Students took turns rotating through one of two assignments each week where they could receive feedback from instructor and classmates. For one assignment, students identified and labeled palpation landmarks on a partner volunteer, which they photographed and submitted to the instructor. They received private instructor feedback on landmark palpation accuracy.

A second, video-based assignment incorporated all components of the CoI model, most notably social presence. In it, students made short self-videos demonstrating palpation on a partner that was shared using a class weblog (blog). The class blog, hosted on Google Blogger, was private and restricted to members of the course. An outside blog platform was chosen for ease of use, especially for embedding video, as compared to the university learning management system. In addition, the class blog remained available as a resource to students after the course ended. The entire class had authorship allowing them to post and comment freely.

Classmates were required to watch each other's videos and give feedback comments to one classmate weekly. Peer coaching has been found to improve psychomotor skill development in nursing students (Himes & Ravert, 2012). An instructor gave feedback comments to all videos using a feedback guideline that included dimensions of communication, positioning, body mechanics, draping, technique, accuracy, and time management. All posts and feedback comments (students' and instructor's) were visible to all members of the class blog.

A shared blog allows collaborative online learning between presenter and audience, enhances social presence, and can positively affect student learning (De Jong, Savin-Baden, Cunningham, & Verstegen, 2014; Fluckiger, Vigil, Pasco, & Danielson, 2010; Huang, Huang, & Yu, 2011; Means et al., 2013; Tan, Ladyshewsky, & Gardner, 2010). Blogs also overcome some face-to-face classroom limitations like space shortages, time constraints, and student anxiety about evaluating peer work (Huang et al., 2011). Student-class-instructor interaction in the class blog also allows peer benchmarking that can improve student self-assessment and understanding of performance expectations (Maloney, Storr, Paynter, et al., 2013).

FACE-TO-FACE CLASSROOM

With all skills introduced and practiced online, face-to-face lab time was used for refinement and mastery of palpation skills in preparation for practical skills assessment. During a 3-hour lab session, students rotated through stations supervised by lab instructors who reviewed content and gave hands-on feedback. An optional, unstructured practice time was available to students outside of class with a lab assistant present to answer questions.

Each on-campus institute ended with a practical skills assessment of psychomotor learning. performance dimensions, as in the video assignment, were proper techniques, body mechanics, positioning, draping, accuracy, communication, and time management. The fourth and final skills check was cumulative.

OUTCOMES

Subjects were 123 first-year DPT students (71 females) from three successive cohorts spanning 2012-2014 (cohorts A, B, C respectively). Outcomes were analyzed including (a) student performance scores on practical skills assessments, (b) online engagement rates, and (c) student course evaluations. Performance scores and engagement rates were analyzed using descriptive statistics. Course evaluation rating scores were analyzed using descriptive statistics and comments were thematically analyzed. One subject of the 2014 cohort withdrew from the university at the beginning of the course and these data were removed from analysis.

ONLINE PARTICIPATION
AND ENGAGEMENT

As a measure of student engagement in the online lab activity, counts of student blog page views, blog posts, and comments were collected from the blog statistics page. Students met posting requirements with few exceptions. Students exceeded the required/expected number of peer comments and page views at a rate of roughly double the comments and 8–10 times the page views (see Table 1).

STUDENT PERFORMANCE

Practical skills assessments required that students perform palpation skills on a preselected set of palpation landmarks drawn at random. Performance was scored using a score sheet that captured performance dimension like those of the video assignment on a binary met/not-met scale. The score sheet was created by the lead faculty,

a physical therapist, who was board certified in orthopedic physical therapy and a certified clinical instructor. It was used in its original form with a preceding cohort and refined with input from other faculty subject matter experts. While no formal validity testing was performed, the development process gives the score sheet increased face and construct validity. To improve score reliability, it was standard practice for course faculty to meet after testing and to reach consensus on any points of concern or disagreement in grading. Seventy-five was set as a passing score as per HDPT program policy. The range of median performance scores was high but narrow (see Table 2). Among the three cohorts, only one failing score on a skills check was recorded.

COURSE EVALUATIONS
AND STUDENT PERCEPTIONS

Online course evaluation surveys were completed anonymously online. The response rate was 100% as it is a university requirement. The survey contained space for open commenting and six scored sections: course organization, course activities, grading, preparation of course material, delivery of instruction, and student-instructor interactions. Each section contained 5–7 items ranked on a 4-point Likert scale (1 = *strongly disagree* to 4 = *strongly agree*). Sections with items that most related to the CoI model included course organization, preparation of course material, course activities, and student-instructor interaction. Survey items mostly pertained to instructor presence and were completely lacking in items pertaining to social presence. Rankings in all sections were consistently high over the 3-year period. Mean section rankings ranged from 3.56–3.93 and median score for all sections was 4.0 (see Table 3).

Students gave feedback in two open comment sections on the course evaluations pertaining to the overall course and

Table 1. Blog Engagement

	Cohort		
Engagement With Blog	A (n = 39)	B (n = 39)	C (n = 45)
Page views per student per week	10	8.3	10.1
Original post rate for cohort (percent of required)	100%	98%	99%
Commenting rate for cohort (percent of required)	182%	199%	186%

Note: Engagement values based on actual counts obtained from blog corrected for instructor activity. Engagement rates reported as a percentage of actual activity as compared to expected activity based on assignment instructions/requirements.

Table 2. Student Performance on Skills Assessments

	Cohort		
Student Performance (%)	A (n = 39)	B (n = 39)	C (n = 45)
Skill Assessment 1	98.00 (88–100)	86.00 (65–91)	86.00 (74–91)
Skill Assessment 2	98.00 (89–100)	93.50 (78–100)	96.00 (82–100)
Skill Assessment 3	98.00 (91–100)	95.00 (87–100)	97.00 (89–99)
Skill Assessment 4 (cumulative)	96.67 (91–100)	95.79 (78–99)	96.97 (81–99)
Final Course Grade	97.85 (93–100)	91.53 (78–94)	96.50 (91–99)

Note: Student performance score reported as median (range).

Table 3. Course Evaluation Section Scores

	Cohort			
Course Evaluation Section	A (n = 39)	B (n = 39)	C (n = 45)	3-Year Mean
Course Organization	3.64, 0.84	3.83, 0.58	3.57. 0.86	3.68
Course Activities	3.69, 0.73	3.84, 0.54	3.58, 0.80	3.70
Grading	3.68, 0.73	3.80, 0.56	3.56, 0.82	3.68
Preparation of Course Material	3.80, 0.56	3.93, 0.25	3.64, 0.79	3.79
Delivery of Instruction	3.77, 0.58	3.89, 0.31	3.62, 0.80	3.76
Student-Instructor Interaction	3.76, 0.58	3.89, 0.25	3.62, 0.79	3.76
Overall mean score				

Note: Section items ranked on a 4-point Likert Scale: 1 = *strongly disagree*; 2 = *disagree*; 3 = *agree*; 4 = *strongly agree*. Section values reported as mean, standard deviation.

to the lead instructor. One hundred and five comments were reviewed and thematically coded (see Table 4). Six themes emerged from the comments: student satisfaction/engagement, teaching presence—course design, teaching presence—responsiveness, cognitive presence, social presence, and assessment. The most common comments pertained to satisfaction/engagement with the course and included descriptors such as, "fun," "excellent," "enjoyed," and "favorite."

Table 4. Course Evaluation Comment Themes

Themes	Descriptors (Comment Count)
Satisfaction/engagement	General positive comments (33)
Teaching presence–course design	Organization, expectations, time management, instruction (33)
Teaching presence—responsiveness	Feedback and face-to-face interaction (21)
Cognitive presence	Learning, hands-on practice, and course assignments (24)
Social presence	Peer interaction and peer benchmarking (5)
Assessment	Grader consistency and fairness (5)

Note: Major themes with comment descriptors from analysis of comments of three successive cohorts.

Comments in the teaching presence—course design theme referred to being well organized, having clear expectations, aiding time management, and instruction (see Table 4). The comments were generally positive. One student wrote "I felt like I knew what was expected of me ahead of time, and I had ample time to prepare." Another wrote, "there were no surprises." Another commented that he/she "felt prepared for ... institute and institute felt more like a review." Some constructive feedback was given regarding videos and face-to-face time. One student suggested that videos be more detailed and descriptive, and another suggested more instructor-made videos, versus the text companion DVD. While comments were largely positive regarding face-to-face instruction, four students felt that the time was too short and one felt it was too long.

Teaching presence—responsiveness theme comments related to feedback and face-to-face interaction. Comments about both formative and summative feedback online and face-to-face were very common and largely positive (see Table 4). Some students also commented positively on the timeliness of feedback, highlighting the temporal quality of this theme. Further, students commented about a period when feedback was unavailable due to a technical problem. Some gave constructive feedback in this theme pertaining to perceived variability between online instruction (text and video), face-to-face instruction (in lab), and between individual lab assistants in lab.

The cognitive presence theme emerged with comments related to learning, hands-on practice, and course assignments (see Table 4). Comments in this theme support positive student learning perceptions in both online and face-to-face modes. Some commented that assignments and varied media enhanced learning, with one student noting a preference for video over photo assignments and another writing that "the video blog is a great idea." One student commented that he or she "learned the most in class on institute weekends"; however, three students referred to "hands-on" learning as a positive aspect of the course despite being largely taught online at a distance. This paradox is underscored by the comment "never knew that I can [sic] learn palpation online!"

Social presence was not measured in the course evaluation survey, but was evident in student comments. While not as prevalent, comments about peer interaction and peer benchmarking emerged as a social presence theme (see Table 4). Several students commented positively on the use of videos and a blog as an assignment platform that allowed for interaction. One student commented "I liked having the opportunity to get feedback from ... classmates on a weekly basis." Another student reflected peer benchmarking in the comment, "I really like being able to see what my classmates are doing in their videos." No constructive feedback was given in this theme area, except the feedback that video assignments were preferred to photo assignments. It is not known if the lack of social presence survey items affected contributed to the lack of open comments offered.

The final theme, assessments, emerged in comments about course assessments and their scoring (see Table 4). These comments were split. Two students commented that assessments were "fair," while three students commented on perceived inconsistencies between graders. These three comments came only from cohort B, but are consistent with comments about variation between instructors in the face-to-face lab.

DISCUSSION AND CONCLUSION

It is common perception that psychomotor physical therapy skills must be learned with the instructor and students working together in the same lab, classroom, or clinic. Rather, 75% of the instruction in a psychomotor physical therapy course was successfully taught to distant learners challenging the notion that while educational technologies are effective supplements to traditional teaching, they could not be a replacement for them (Arroyo-Morales et al., 2012; Davies, Ramsay, Lindfield, & Couperthwaite, 2005). While technologies have demonstrated benefit to student learning outcomes and student perceptions, their ability to replace face-to-face class time has not been a focus in PT education research. This case report describes the hybrid redesign of a traditional course using the CoI model. The outcomes demonstrate a significant savings in face-to-face instructional time with favorable learning outcomes and student satisfaction.

Students generally have positive perceptions of using educational technology and blended approaches. Accessibility, flexibility, and time to reflect and prepare are positive features of the hybrid course design (Garrison & Vaughn, 2008). In a hybrid course, promoting student engagement online is an important factor because of competing time and attention demands outside a physical classroom and fewer ways to connect when at a distance (Meyer, 2014). Tools such as blogs, that facilitate and enhance student-teacher interaction, establish social presence, which improves outcomes and empower students in their learning (Kliger & Pfeiffer, 2011; Means, Toyama, Murphy, Bakia, & Jones, 2010; Rowe, Bozalek, & Frantz, 2013). In this case, a course blog served as a virtual meeting place to reduce social and psychological distance between course members, which is a positive predictor of student perception of learning and satisfaction (Meyer, 2014).

There were limited constructive or negative comments received across three cohorts of feedback. What was received related to instructional variations between instructors face-to-face, between feedback online versus face-to-face, or between graders during assessments. Attempts were made proactively to standardize instructed skills; however, there exists technique variation among physical therapists, often with several correct ways to perform a skill. These student comments may be a function of the novice learner not yet comfortable reconciling this variability. More thorough qualitative methodology such as focus groups may be better suited to generate constructive feedback in future research.

In contrast to other studies, technology was not found to be a detractor, barrier, or consideration for participants in this course (Button, Harrington, & Belan, 2014; Dejong et al., 2014; Hayward, 2004; Kliger & Pfeiffer, 2011). In this case, the sample was comprised of students enrolled in a program delivered entirely in hybrid format. As such, participants have an expectation of heavy technology use and may be more technology literate and tolerant.

While student satisfaction and engagement is desirable, alone it gives limited insight into the achievement of desired learning outcomes. In the current study, student learning outcomes were favorable across three cohorts. Without a comparison group, it is impossible to assert superiority of any teaching method based on these results. In a systematic review with meta-analysis, hybrid education was found more effective than traditional or online-only education (Means et al., 2010). This may be because of the varied instructional techniques, expanded learning time, and space to practice and reflect that this delivery method affords (Garrison & Vaughn, 2008; Means et al., 2010). Course activities that included peer-to-peer feedback facilitate independence in learning (Asghar, 2010; Bayliss & Warden, 2011; Himes & Ravert, 2012; Moore, Westwater-Wood, & Kerry, 2016). Creating self-videos facilitates improved performance on assessments by promoting self-critique and reflection-on-action through attention to performance, behaviors, and mannerisms (Maloney, Storr, Morgan, et al., 2013; Maloney, Storr, Paynter, et al., 2013; Stephens & Parr, 2013).

The three elements of the CoI model used to design the course were evident in course feedback. In contrast to the basic three elements of the model, four themes emerged from student comments reflecting two subthemes of teacher presence: course design and responsiveness (Carlon et al., 2012). Course design relates to matters of organization, clear instruction, tool selection, and planning assignments that support student learning through sound pedagogical choices (Dejong et al., 2014; Meyer, 2014). Responsiveness, related to instructor behaviors and timeliness of communication, are positive predictors of student perceptions and improve outcomes (Kliger & Pfeiffer, 2011; Meyer, 2014).

Social presence was the weakest theme to emerge from student comments, but was evidenced by blog participation rates. It is noteworthy that the course feedback survey lacked items related to social presence, which may have contributed to its underrepresentation in the comments. Alternatively, perhaps components of the course design intended to create social presence were not sufficient or social connection in the online portion of the course is not a priority for this sample of students who see each other monthly. More in-depth investigation is needed to address this question, but the current research will be used to inform revisions to the course feedback survey to better evaluate social presence in future HDPT courses.

Analysis of faculty outcomes was not part of this case; however, faculty are a pivotal component of hybrid course delivery. The initial design of a hybrid course and online set-up requires considerable time, skill, and resources (Button et al., 2014; Pittinger & Olson-Kellogg, 2012; Rowe et al., 2013). Care must be taken to identify quality instructional materials or produce them when unavailable. Once established, faculty technology literacy, overarching support from administration, and technology support staff are potential barriers (Meyer, 2014; Phillips, Forbes, & Duke, 2013). While flexible, time demands are considerable and hybrid delivery may not decrease faculty time, but merely change when and how time is spent. In this case, time spent tending to the online course ranged from 5-6 hours per week (for a 1-credit hour lab course). More study is needed to realistically analyze the workload and resource demands of blended teaching models.

This case report has several limitations. The context of the described course is uniquely situated within a completely hybrid-delivered DPT program. This may limit generalizability and potentially introduces selection bias. Participant students, faculty, and administration involved have the expectation of heavy technology use and results may not be easily reproduced in another curricular context. Validity, reliability, and precision of the skill assessment instrument is not known and grader variation was one of the negative comments received from students. The grading instrument was created and tested in an iterative process by a team of content experts, which gives face and content validity at best. Attempts to improve reliability were made by training proctors to use the instrument, maintaining a consistent pool of graders across assessments, and conducting postassessment discussion to clarify and standardize scoring by consensus. Scoring subjectivity was reduced by scoring criteria based on a met/not-met scale, but this reduced measurement sensitivity and contributed to the low stratification of assessment grades.

More in-depth qualitative analysis including focus groups is needed to explore possible constructive feedback or negative perceptions. Further quantitative research is needed to compare outcomes of psychomotor objectives taught with hybrid versus traditional teaching methods to support the most effective and efficient teaching methods.

Despite the prevailing traditional model for the instruction of psychomotor skills, this case report suggests that hybrid delivery is capable of achieving satisfactory outcomes with a substantial reduction of face-to-face time. Purposeful course redesign using the CoI framework, sound pedagogical principles, and supportive technology that did not supersede pedagogy was used to create a rich online lab environment that complemented a face-to-face lab classroom.

Strategies described in this case report have been adopted and adapted for use in other courses in the HDPT program with psychomotor and affective skills.

REFERENCES

Arroyo-Morales, M., Cantarero-Villanueva, I., Fernández-Lao, C., Guirao-Piñeyro, M., Castro-Martín, E., & Díaz-Rodríguez, L. (2012). A blended learning approach to palpation and ultrasound imaging skills through supplementation of traditional classroom teaching with an e-learning package. *Manual Therapy, 17*(5), 474–478. https://doi.org/10.1016/j.math.2012.04.002

Asghar, A. M. (2010). Reciprocal peer coaching and its use as a formative assessment strategy for first-year students. *Assessment & Evaluation in Higher Education, 35*(4), 403–417. https://doi.org/10.1080/02602930902862834

Bayliss, A. J., & Warden, S. J. (2011). A hybrid model of student-centered instruction improved physical therapist student performance in cardiopulmonary practice patterns by enhancing performance in higher cognitive domains. *Journal of Physical Therapy Education, 25*(3), 14–20. Retrieved from http://www.aptaeducation.org/members/jopte/index.cfm

Boucher, B., Robertson, E., Wainner, R., & Sanders, B. (2013). "Flipping" Texas State University's physical therapist musculoskeletal curriculum: Implementation of a hybrid learning model. *Journal of Physical Therapy Education, 27*(3), 72–77. Retrieved from http://www.aptaeducation.org/members/jopte/index.cfm

Brandt, B. F., Quake-Rapp, C., Shanedling, J., Spannaus-Martin, D., & Martin, P. (2010). Blended learning: Emerging best practices in allied health workforce development. *Journal of Allied Health, 39*(4), e167-e172. Retrieved from http://www.asahp.org/journal-of-allied-health/

Button, D., Harrington, A., & Belan, I. (2014). E-learning & information communication technology (ICT) in nursing education: A review of the literature. *Nurse Education Today, 34*(2014), 1311–1323. https://doi.org/10.1016/j.nedt.2013.05.002

Cain, D. L., & Pitre, P. E. (2008). The effect of computer mediated conferencing and computer assisted instruction on student learning outcomes. *Journal of Asynchronous Learning Networks, 12*(3–4), 31–52. Retrieved from https://secure.onlinelearningconsortium.org/publications/olj_main

Carlon, S., Bennett-Woods, D., Berg, B., Claywell, L., LeDuc, K, … Zenoni, L. (2012). The community of inquiry instrument: Validation and results in online health care disciplines. *Computers & Education, 59*(2012), 215–

221. https://doi.org/10.1016/j.compedu.2012.01.004

Coffee, J. A., & Hillier, S. (2008). Teaching precursor clinical skills using an online audiovisual tool: An evaluation using student responses. *MERLOT Online Journal of Learning and Teaching, 4*(4), 8. Retrieved from http://jolt.merlot.org/vol4no4/coffee_1208.pdf

Davies A., Ramsay J., Lindfield, H., & Couperthwaite, J. (2005). A blended approach to learning: Added value and lessons learnt from students' use of computer-based materials for neurological analysis. *British Journal of Educational Technology, 35*(5), 839–849. https://doi.org/10.1111/j.1467-8535.2005.00506.x

De Jong, N., Savin-Baden, M., Cunningham, A. M., & Verstegen, D. M. L. (2014). Blended learning in health education: Three case studies. *Perspectives in Medical Education, 3*, 278–288. https://doi.org/10.0007/s40037-014-0108-1

Fluckiger, J., Vigil, Y. T., Pasco, R., & Danielson, K. (2010). Formative feedback: Involving students as partners in assessment to enhance learning. *College Teaching, 58*(4), 136–140. http://doi.org/10.1080/87567555.2010.484031

Gaida, J. J., Seville, C., Cope, L., Dalwood, N., Morgan, P., & Maloney, S. (2016). Acceptability of a blended learning model that improves student readiness for practical skill learning: A mixed-methods study. *Focus on Health Professional Education, 17*(1), 3–17. https://doi.org/10.11157/fohpe.v17i1.116

Gardner, P., Slater, H., Jordan, J. E., Fary, R. E., Chua, J., & Briggs, A. M. (2016). Physiotherapy students' perspectives of online e-learning for interdisciplinary management of chronic health conditions: A qualitative study. *BMC Medical Education, 16*(62), 1–9. https://doi.org/10.1186/s12909-016-0593-5

Garrison, D.R. & Vaughan, N.D. (2008). *Blended learning in higher education: Framework, principles, and guidelines.* San Francisco, CA: Jossey-Bass.

Garrison, D. R., Anderson, T., & Archer, W. (2010). The first decade of the community of inquiry framework: A retrospective. *Internet & Higher Education, 13*(1/2), 5–9. http://dx.doi.org/10.1016/j.iheduc.2009.10.003

George, P. P., Papachristou, N., Belisario, J. M., Wang, W., Wark, P. A., Cotic, Z., … Car, J. (2014). Online eLearning for undergraduates in health professions: A systematic review of the impact on knowledge, skills, attitudes and satisfaction. *Journal of Global Health, 4*(1), 1–17. https://doi.org/10.7189/jogh.04.010406

Hayward, L. M. (2004). Integrating web-enhanced instruction into a research methods course: examination of student experiences and perceived learning. *Journal of Physical Therapy Education, 18*(2), 54–65. Retrieved from http://www.aptaeducation.org/members/jopte/index.cfm

Himes, D. O., & Ravert, P. K. (2012). Situated peer coaching and unfolding cases in the fundamentals skills laboratory. *International Journal of Nursing Education Scholarship, 9*(1), 1–19. https://doi.org/10.1515/1548-923X.2335

Huang, T.-C., Huang, Y.-M., & Yu, F.-Y. (2011). Cooperative weblog learning in higher education: Its facilitating effects on social interaction, time lag, and cognitive load. *Educational Technology & Society, 14*(1), 95–106. Retrieved from http://www.ifets.info/journals/14_1/9.pdf

Hurst, K. M. (2016). Using video podcasting to enhance the learning of clinical skills: A qualitative study of physiotherapy students' experiences. *Nurse Education Today, 45*, 206–211. https://doi.org/10.1016/j.nedt.2016.08.011

Kliger, D., & Pfeiffer, E. (2011). Engaging students in blended courses through increased technology. *Journal of Physical Therapy Education, 25*(1), 11–14. Retrieved from http://www.aptaeducation.org/members/jopte/index.cfm

Maloney, S., Storr, M., Morgan, P., & Ilic, D. (2013). The effect of student self-video of performance on clinical skill competency: A randomised controlled trial. *Advances In Health Sciences Education: Theory and Practice, 18*(1), 81-89. http://dx.doi.org/10.1007/s10459-012-9356-1

Maloney, S., Storr, M., Paynter, S., Morgan, P., & Ilic, D. (2013). Investigating the efficacy of practical skill teaching: A pilot-study comparing three educational methods. *Advances in Health Sciences Education: Theory and Practice, 18*(1), 71–80. http://dx.doi.org/10.1007/s10459-012-9355-2

Means, B., Toyama, Y., Murphy, R., & Baki, M. (2013). The effectiveness of online and blended learning: A meta-analysis of the empirical literature. *Teachers College Record, 115*(3), 1–47. Retrieved from http://www.tcrecord.org/content.asp?contentid=16882

Meyer, K. A. (2014). Student engagement in online learning: What works and why. *Association for the Study of Higher Education Higher Education Report, 40*(6), 1–114. https://doi.org/10.1002/aehe.20018

Moore, C., Westwater-Wood, S., & Kerry, R. (2016). Academic performance and perception of learning following a peer coaching teaching and assessment strategy. *Advances in Health Sciences Education: Theory And Practice, 21*(1), 121–130. https://doi.org/10.1007/s10459-015-9618-9

Murray, L., McCallum, C., & Petrosino, C. (2014). Flipping the classroom experience: A comparison of online learning to traditional lecture. *Journal of Physical Therapy Education, 28*(3), 35-41. Retrieved from http://www.aptaeducation.org/members/jopte/index.cfm

Phillips, D., Forbes, H., Duke, M. (2013). Teaching and learning innovations for postgraduate education in nursing. *Collegian, 20*(3), 145-151. https://doi.org/10.1016/j.colegn.2012.05.003

Pittenger, A. A., & Olson-Kellogg, B. (2012). Leveraging learning technologies for collaborative writing in an online pharmacotherapy course. *Distance Education, 33*(1), 61–80. https://doi.org/10.1080/01587919.2012.667960

Preston, E., Ada, L., Dean, C. M., Stanton, R., Waddington, G., & Canning, C. (2012). The Physiotherapy eSkills Training Online resource improves performance of practical skills: a controlled trial. *BMC Medical Education, 12*(119), 1–7. https://doi.org/10.1186/1472-6920-12-119

Rasmussen, K., Belisario, J. M., Wark, P. A., Molina, J. A., Loong, S. L., Cotic, Z., ... Car, J. (2014). Offline eLearning for undergraduates in health professions: A systematic review of the impact on knowledge, skills, attitudes and satisfaction. *Journal of Global Health, 4*(1), 0–18. https://doi.org/10.7189/jogh.04.010405

Rowe, M., Bozalek, V., & Frantz, J. (2013). Using Google Drive to facilitate a blended approach to authentic learning. *British Journal of Educational Technology, 44*(4), 594–606. https://doi.org/10.1111/bjet.12063

Stephens, J., & Parr, M. (2013). The development of media-driven clinical skills through using the "e-skills portfolio." *International Journal of Therapy & Rehabilitation, 20*(7), 336–342. https://doi.org/10.12968/ijtr.2013.20.7.336

Tan, S. M., Ladyshewsky, R. R., & Gardner, P. (2010). Using blogging to promote clinical reasoning and metacognition in undergraduate physiotherapy fieldwork programs. *Australasian Journal of Educational Technology, 26*(3), 355–368. https://doi.org/10.14742/ajet.1080

Van Duijn, A. J., Swanick, K., & Donald, E. K. (2014). Student learning of cervical psychomotor skills via online video instruction versus traditional face-to-face instruction. *Journal of Physical Therapy Education, 28*(1), 94–102. Retrieved from http://www.aptaeducation.org/members/jopte/index.cfm

Veneri, D. (2011). The role and effectiveness of computer-assisted learning in physical therapy education: A systematic review. *Physiotherapy Theory & Practice, 27*(4), 287–298. http://dx.doi.org/10.3109/09593985.2010.493192

Veneri, D. A., & Gannotti, M. (2014). A comparison of student outcomes in a physical therapy neurologic rehabilitation course based on delivery mode: Hybrid vs traditional. *Journal of Allied Health, 43*(4), e75–e81. Retrieved from http://www.asahp.org/journal-of-allied-health/

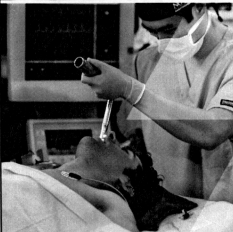

Student Perceptions of Factors Influencing Success in Hybrid and Traditional DPT Programs
A Q-Sort Analysis

Lance Cherry and Mary Blackinton

BACKGROUND AND PURPOSE

Hybrid learning, the blend of online and face-to-face learning experiences, is a novel but rapidly expanding instructional approach in physical therapist education. Our Hybrid Doctor of Physical Therapy (H-DPT) program was designed to provide flexibility for working adults and those with geographic or financial constraints. In the H-DPT Program, students learn via online instruction for 3 weeks followed by 4 days (32-36 hours) of intensive face-to-face learning on-campus each month. During the 3 weeks of online instruction, students watch screen-captured lectures and vid-

Lance Cherry,
Associate Professor, Department of Physical Therapy, Nova Southeastern University-Tampa, 3632 Queen Palm Drive, Tampa, FL 33619.
Telephone: (813) 574-5327.
E-mail: lc1315@nova.edu

Mary Blackinton,
Associate Professor, Department of Physical Therapy, Nova Southeastern University, 3632 Queen Palm Drive, Tampa, FL 33619.
Telephone: (813) 574-5311.
E-mail: maryb@nova.edu

eos, practice skills, upload videos of themselves performing skills to web-based platforms such as blogs, receive feedback from peers and faculty, take quizzes, read texts, and submit assignments related to course content. Most learning activities occur at self-selected times asynchronously, although there are occasional synchronous activities such as web-based meetings. All courses have weekly deadlines for assignments and quizzes. The 4 days of face-to-face instruction consists of psychomotor skill practice accompanied by immediate feedback, honing clinical reasoning and problem-solving skills, applying material learned in lecture-based courses (debates, journal clubs), and taking high-stakes practical and written exams.

Garrison and Vaughan (2008) refer to blended learning as the "thoughtful fusion of online and face-to-face experiences" (p. 5). Hybrid instruction is a distinct instructional modality. It is distinct from traditional classrooms, where all instruction is done face to face; it is different than online courses, where all instruction is done online: and it is dissimilar to "flipped" classrooms, where there is a shift in passive learning activities (lectures) to online while bringing application (case studies) into the classroom (Berrett, 2012; Boucher, Robertson, Wainner, & Sanders, 2013; Murray, McCallum, & Petrosino, 2014; Wong & Chu, 2014). While some researchers evaluated factors influencing student success or retention in online and blended environments (Smith, 2005; Smith, Murphy, & Mahoney, 2003), none to date have investigated factors impacting success in hybrid DPT programs. It is also unclear if there are differences in student perceptions regarding what factors impact student success in traditional versus hybrid DPT programs.

Academic success can be viewed through a variety of lenses. Alexander Astin (2012) suggests that student outcomes (O) are a result of "inputs" (I) or personal qualities that students bring to the educational experience (academic achieve-

ment, study behaviors, aspiration, financial status, life goals), as well as "environment" (E) factors that the students experience during the academic experience (program policies, curriculum, facilities, instructors, friends, family support, teaching styles). This "IEO" model reflects the milieu of factors impacting student outcomes.

Similarly, Rovai's persistence model in distance education distinguishes preadmission variables such as student characteristics (academic preparation, age, ethnicity) and student skills (computer literacy, time management) from postadmission variables such as learning community, interpersonal relationships, study habits, advising, teaching/learning styles, finances, hours of employment, and family responsibilities (Rovai, 2003). In physical therapy education, predictors of academic success have been analyzed using student inputs prior to and during the professional curriculum such as grade point average and standardized exam scores (Kosmahl, 2005), as well as program variables such as accreditation status, number of faculty with PhD or EdD degrees, and total years of preprofessional and professional coursework (Mohr, Ingram, Hayes, & Du, 2005).

In the context of blended learning environments, Garrison and Vaughan (2008) describe a community of inquiry framework depicting factors that influence learning in blended classrooms. This framework describes three realms influencing student learning in the hybrid classroom: social presence, cognitive presence, and teaching presence. Social presence refers to the personal communication and camaraderie between students and between students and faculty; cognitive presence is the exploration and exchange of information and new ideas; and teaching presence refers to the educational design, direction, and focus created by the instructor (Garrison & Vaughan, 2008). These elements, in addition to those variables put forth by Astin and Rovai, suggest there are many variables that could influence student success in a hybrid DPT program.

Student perceptions of variables impacting success have been investigated in health professions education, although not related to online or hybrid programs specifically. A qualitative study investigated factors influencing academic achievement in high achieving medical students (Abdulghani et al., 2014). Using focus groups and grounded theory analysis, the researchers identified four primary themes related to academic success: learning strategies, resource management, motivation, and dealing with nonacademic problems (Abdulghani et al., 2014). These four themes were further broken down into 17 subthemes, such as lecture attendance, prioritization of learning needs, mind mapping, and learning from mistakes (learning strategy theme), time management and family support (resource management theme), internal motivation and exam results (motivation), and language barriers, homesickness, and stress (dealing with non-academic problem theme).

Similarly, student perceptions of dental school including morale, strengths and challenges, and ranking of content area importance were researched using a survey of students from five western dental schools (Cardall, 2008). The findings from over 740 student participants revealed the top five positive influences on their school experience included faculty, clinical experiences, classmates, curriculum, and facilities; whereas the most frequent negative experiences related to curriculum, clinical experience, organization, student/faculty ratio, and patient pool (Cardall, 2008). Interestingly, clinical experience and the curriculum were viewed as both positive and negative influences.

In summary, there is a dearth of literature in physical therapy education regarding factors students believe to influence success, and little to no literature describing such beliefs related to hybrid education in the health professions or specific to physical therapy.

The overarching purpose of this investigation was to determine students' perceptions of factors they believe influence their success in a hybrid DPT program and to compare their perceptions with students in a traditional DPT program. Understanding students' beliefs about success is analogous to understanding patients' health beliefs. By identifying student perceptions about success, programs can potentially identify potential barriers and facilitators in designing hybrid classrooms and curricula, improve the admissions selection process to better match applicants with the hybrid program, share findings with prospective applicants to improve their understanding of the program, and assist faculty who advise students.

METHODOLOGY

SUBJECTS

Following institutional review board approval, subjects were recruited from two programs within one university—a hybrid DPT program and a traditional DPT program. Students were recruited verbally and via email. No incentives or rewards were provided to participants.

IDENTIFICATION OF VARIABLES

Based on a review of the literature regarding students' perception of success in online/hybrid education and in health professions education, we identified variables potentially impacting student success (Rovai, 2003; Park & Choi, 2009; Smith, 2005; Smith et al., 2005). Our goal was to include variables related to both the individual student (I) and educational environment (E) as described in Astin's work. We also wanted to ensure that E variables reflected all areas the community of inquiry model (Garrison & Vaughan, 2008) for hybrid learning: social, instructor, and

Table 1. Student Variables Identified Through Literature Review and Organized by Astin's IEO Model and the Community of Inquiry Model

Individual Student Characteristics		Educational Characteristics		
Student Attributes/ Skills	Student External Variables	Social Presence	Instructor Presence	Cognitive Presence
• Academic work ethic • Beliefs about teaching and learning • Self-confidence in learning • Self-initiative in learning • Prior academic performance (grades) • Preadmission major (study area) • Previous work experience • Ability to filter large amounts of information • Ability to prioritize study focus • Computer literacy • Ability to search information online • Time management • Reading skills • Writing skills • Problem-solving skills	• Finances • Hours worked per week • Family demands • Outside support and encouragement • Life crises	• Collaboration with peers online • Collaboration with peers face to face • Access to student services • Social peer interaction • Peer support	• Instructor responsiveness to student needs • Instructor's ability to foster a sense of community • Instructor's ability to organize course material • Instructor's ability to clarify course/assignment expectations • The frequency of instructor interaction • Timeliness of information from instructor • Timeliness of feedback from the instructor	• Degree to which class activities aid reflection and learning • Organization of courses in the curriculum • Types of available course resources (books, videos) • Access to resources outside the classroom (library, physical therapist)

cognitive presence. Three faculty reviewed the variables for face validity, and as a result 36 variables were identified (Table 1).

Q-SORT SURVEY METHODOLOGY

Since this study was conducted to investigate student perceptions of success, we used a descriptive methodology called Q-Sort because it characterizes opinions through comparative rank ordering (Portney & Watkins, 2015). According to Dennis (1986), Q-Sort is particularly valuable in research that explores human perceptions and interpersonal relationships. The Q-Sort procedure requires participants to sort a set of items (in this case, 36 factors influencing their success) into five ordinal categories, ranging from most influential to least influential, regarding student success. The number of items permitted in each category is fixed in advance so the shape of the distribution of item scores is constant for all students and reflects a bell-shaped curve.

PROCEDURES

To begin the Q-Sort, each participant received a set of 36 index cards, each index card describing one variable that potentially influenced student success. Participants were not given an operational definition of success, and if they asked, were told, "whatever you feel is success as a student. Participants were provided a symmetrical bell-shaped grid on poster board consisting of columns numbered one through five; each column representing a different degree of influencing student success (Figure 1). Column 1 was labeled "least influential," column 2 "not very influential," column 3 "somewhat influential," column 4 "very influential," and column 5 "most influential." To maintain a bell-shaped curve suggested for Q-Sort methodology, participants were lim-

ited in the number of cards they could place under each column: 4 cards for "most" and "least" influential, 8 cards in "not very" and "very" influential, and 12 cards in the "somewhat influential" column (Figure 1). Participants were instructed to take as much time as they needed to complete the Q-Sort, placing all 36 cards (variables) in each column as they saw fit. They were also told that the order of the cards (variables) within each column did not matter, just the selection of which column to place each variable. As students finished, they notified the PI or coinvestigator, who then double-checked that all the spaces were filled and no cards were left over.

In order to maintain the appropriate groups for proper data input, the cards from each column were placed in a corre-

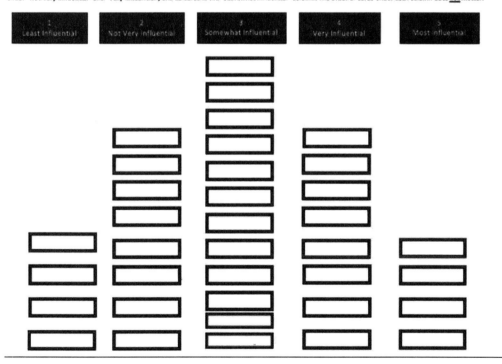

Figure 1.   Q-Sort directions.

sponding envelope marked 1–5. When all cards were placed in envelopes from a particular students' board they were wrapped together with a rubber band and placed in a larger envelope until they were input for data analysis.

DATA ANALYSIS

The Q-Sort analysis looks for correlations between subjects across a sample of variables (Portney & Watkins, 2009), reducing many individual viewpoints of the subjects down to a few factors. The term *factor* in the Q-Sort is defined as representing individuals with similar views, feelings, or experiences (Akhtar-Danesh et al., 2013). In our Q-Sort, factors represent groups of individuals with similar views about which variables influenced student success.

For this study, analysis of the Q-Sorts was conducted using the PQ Method 2.33, a free downloadable software program (Schmolck, 2014). This is the program most recommended by the International Society for the Scientific Study of Subjectivity. The PQ Method is a statistical program tailored to the requirements of Q-Sort studies. Specifically, it allows the user to enter each Q-Sort individually, identifying which variables were selected in each of the 5 columns. The PQ Method program computes inter-correlations among Q-Sorts, which are then factor analyzed and rotated for simplification (Schmolck, 2012). The analysis step produces an extensive report with a variety of tables on factor loadings, statement factor scores, and discriminating statements for each of the factors (Schmolck, 2012).

The number of factors created by the Q-Sort program is based on a correlation matrix between all Q-Sorts followed by factor matrix analysis. Each factor thus had its own set of scores, expressed as z scores for each variable/statement. Since there so many variables represented in each factor, we reported each factor using only those variables with z scores greater than or equal to 1.5 (representing most influential) and less than or equal to –1.5 (representing least influential). The individual statement factor z scores were used to develop an understanding of the profile for each factor and to make comparisons among the factors.

This Q-Sort methodology cannot compare two different data sets (hybrid vs. traditional) directly as one might do in an independent t test. Instead, we entered the data for the H-DPT program and DPT program separately and compared the factors identified by each group.

RESULTS

Two cohorts completed the q-sort: Hybrid DPT Students (H-DPT) and Traditional DPT students (DPT). Results for each q-sort are reported separately based on the way the Q-sorts were analyzed.

HYBRID DPT STUDENTS

Participants. A total of 54 H-DPT students participated, including 20 second-year students and 34 first-year students. Although demographic data were not collected, the average age of the two cohorts combined (based on admission statistics) was 26.2 years, 58% female and 42% male.

Factors. The Q-Sort data from the Hybrid sample created four factors. Again, a factor is a subgroup of responses representing groups of individuals with similar views about which variables influenced student success ranked in a similar manner using correlations. For each of the four factors, the statements with z scores of greater than +1.5 ("strongly impacting success") or less than –1.5 ("least impacting success") are identified (Table 2). Among the statements with z scores of greater than +1.5 (most influencing success), "self-initiation in learning" was identified in all four factors, and "time management" noted in

Table 2. Hybrid Student Factors and Perceptions Rated Most and Least Likely to Impact Success*

Factor	1	2	3	4
# Defining variables	9	9	10	4
Composite reliability coefficient	.97	.97	.98	.94
SE Z scores	.164	.164	.156	.243
Variables most impacting success (z score)	• Self-initiation in learning (1.98) • Ability to prioritize study focus (1.80) • Academic work ethic (1.76) • Time management (1.69)	• Time management (2.2) • Self-initiation in learning (1.78) • Ability to prioritize study focus (1.51)	• Self-initiative in learning (1.81) • Degree class aids reflection and learning (1.65) • Academic work ethic (1.50)	• Time management (1.67) • Instructors ability clarify expectations (1.63) • Self-initiative in learning (1.57)
Variables least impacting success (z score)	• Preadmission major (–1.89) • Finances (–1.80) • Access to student services (–1.57)	• Access to student services (–2.12) • Beliefs about teaching/learning (–1.91)	• Family demands (–2.11) • Beliefs about teaching/ learning (–1.76) • Access to student services (–1.62)	• Instructors ability to foster a sense of community (–2.26) • Social peer interaction (–2.06)

Note: *Based on z scores ±1.5 standard deviations.

three of the four factors, whereas "academic work ethic" and "student ability to identify study focus" were identified in two of the four factors (Table 2). Among the statements with z scores of less than –1.5 (least influencing student success), "access to student services" was identified in three of the four factors, and "beliefs about teaching and learning" was identified in two of the four factors (Table 2).

Consensus Statements. The Q-Sort program identified consensus statements, meaning those statements that did not significantly distinguish one group (factor) from any other group (factor). For the Hybrid program, there were six consensus statements (Table 3). There were three positive consensus statements (students perceived it strongly impacted success) including: "self-initiative in learning," "problem-solving skills, and "organization of courses in the curriculum." There were

also three negative consensus statements (students perceived it did not impact success) including: "prior academic performance," "writing skills" and "access to resources outside the classroom."

TRADITIONAL DPT STUDENTS

Participants. Seventy-one traditional DPT students participated in the Q-Sort. Although demographic data were not collected, the average age of the two cohorts combined (based on admission statistics) was 24.3 years. Gender was not identified in the traditional cohort.

Factors. The Q-Sort data from the Traditional sample created four factors. For traditional students, "time management" was identified as strongly influencing success in three of the four factors, while "academic work ethic" and "ability to prioritize study focus" were identified in two of the

Table 3. Hybrid Student Consensus Statements

Positive Consensus Statements	Negative Consensus Statements
• Self-initiative in learning • Problem-solving skills • Organization of courses in the curriculum	• Prior academic performance (grades) • Writing skills • Access to resources outside the classroom

Table 4. Traditional Student Factors and Perceptions Rated Most and Least Likely to Impact Success

Factor	1	2	3	4
# Defining variables	19	15	9	6
Composite reliability Coefficient	.99	.98	.97	.96
SE Z scores	.114	.128	.164	.200
Variables most impacting success (z score)	• Time management (2.10) • Academic work ethic (1.50)	• Time management (2.07) • Ability to prioritize study focus (1.94)	• Time management (1.95) • Academic work ethic (1.72) • Problem-solving skills (1.69) • Ability to prioritize study focus (1.61)	• Instructor's ability to organize course material (2.19) • Instructor responsiveness to student needs (1.71)
Variables least impacting success (z score)	• Hours worked/week (–2.07) • Finances (–1.97)	• Access to student services (–1.86) • Collaboration with peers online (–1.70)	• Prior academic performance (–1.63) • Social peer interaction (–1.63) • Previous work experience (–1.56)	• Preadmission major (–1.82) • Access to student services (–1.51) • Writing skills (–1.50) • Instructor's ability to foster community (–1.50)

Note: *Based on z scores ± 1.5 standard deviations.

four factors. The statement with the highest positive z score for the traditional group was "instructor's ability to organize course material."

In the Traditional sample, there was little similarity between the four factors in the statements ranked as "least influential" for impacting student success. "Access to student services" was identified by two of the four factors as being among the least influential. No other statements were similar across factors; however, statements with the highest negative z scores were: "hours worked per week," "finances," and "preadmission major."

Consensus Statements. Again, consensus statements are those statements that did not significantly distinguish one group (factor) from any other group (factor). For the traditional group, there were no consensus statements within the four factors, either positive or negative.

DISCUSSION

The purpose of this study was to determine students' perceptions of factors they believe influence their success in a hybrid DPT program and to compare their perceptions with students in a traditional DPT program. The Q-Sort methodology required participants to rank order the most and least important attributes related to their success, forcing them to consider all attributes potentially related to success rather than selecting a single attribute as one might do in survey methodology. In this discussion, factors represent groups of individuals with similar views about which variables influenced student success. The H-DPT and DPT student Q-Sorts were analyzed separately based on the capability of the PQ Method 2.33.

There were several differences between the hybrid and traditional DPT student perceptions. Self-initiation in learning was identified in all four factor groups in the Hybrid program, with z scores ranging from 1.57–1.98; whereas it was not included in any of the four factor groups from the Traditional program. This finding was not surprising, given the nature of hybrid instruction. Although self-directed learning is a characteristic of professionalism in physical therapy (May, Morgan, Lemke, Karst, & Stone, 1995) students in a hybrid program must be self-directed to independently navigate the learning experiences during the online portion of each month. For example, in most traditional programs, students attend classes at set times each week, following the pace of learning set by the instructor. In contrast, students in a hybrid program access online lectures and videos at self-selected times and a self-selected pace. Further, in our hybrid program, students have weekly assignments to keep them engaged and must then be self-directed to complete the assignments on time.

Another difference between the hybrid and traditional DPT students' perceptions of success was the perceived role of the instructor. In the traditional DPT cohort, one of the four factor groups included "instructor's ability to organize course material," whereas none of the four factor groups in the H-DPT program included this variable. In fact, the highest z score for the traditional DPT students across all factor groups was this variable. Although it was only a factor in one traditional DPT factor group, it may indicate that some traditional DPT students perceive the instructor's organizational skills in organizing class material as being more important than their own attributes.

In contrast, three of the four factor groups in both the Hybrid and Traditional students identified time management as a variable strongly impacting success. Given the intensive nature of physical therapist education, this was not surprising. These findings are like those reported by Abdulghani et al. (2014) in medical students. It is possible that the reasons why time management was rated as strongly influencing success may be different between students in each program. For example, most hybrid DPT students juggle work/family along with school demands, while the traditional students manage a more-intensive course load and must be on-campus every day. Time management is an attribute however that all DPT students emphasized, and this should be shared with prospective students in all programs.

Two variables, "academic work ethic" and "ability to prioritize study focus" were identified as strongly impacting success by two of the four factor groups in both cohorts. These findings are similar to prior research for online learning identified study habits as an important post-admission variable impacting student retention (Rovai, 2003; Smith, 2005).

Consensus statements are those statements that did not significantly distinguish one group (factor) from any other group (factor). Interestingly, the Hybrid cohort had six consensus statements while the Traditional cohort had none. One reason for this difference might be the shared experience of being in a hybrid DPT program. While all students have had similar experiences in traditional classrooms, few students in the Hybrid program had previous exposure to hybrid learning. The uniqueness of being in a hybrid program may have more strongly shaped their perceptions related to what it takes to be successful. For example, DPT students in traditional programs use the same learning strategies they've employed prior to PT school, whereas hybrid DPT students were potentially forced to develop new or different strategies. Further, their experience was unusual or different than most other professional programs, and so they may be more aware or reflective of factors impacting success.

The three consensus statements rated as strongly related to success in all hybrid factor groups included: self-initiative in learning, problem-solving skills, and organization of courses in the curriculum. As stated previously, the importance of self-initiation as an attribute makes sense in a hybrid curriculum because students must organize, plan, and engage in learning on their own time frame. Problem-solving may have been rated consistently high across all factor groups for several reasons. First, the technology itself is an area in which students must problem-solve in online and hybrid environments (Kowalczyk, 2014; Stott & Moser, 2016; Talcott, O'Donnell, & Burns, 2013). For example, in the hybrid program, students must create and upload videos demonstrating a psychomotor skill, and can encounter problems uploading the video in a correct file format to the course management system. It is also possible that time management issues, clearly identified in this study, require problem-solving to decide how to prioritize study and work time. Also, in the H-DPT program, students have more graded assignments than in the Traditional program. When students encounter questions about the assignment or pertaining to

the lecture, they are free to contact faculty; however, many first try to problem-solve on their own before emailing or calling faculty. This is different than being in a classroom where students can raise their hand and easily get a question answered.

There are several limitations of this study. First, the population from which the sample was drawn represents only those students in one university, albeit two distinct programs, so findings cannot be generalized to other programs. Second, students volunteered to participate in the study, meaning they may be those individuals with stronger feelings/perceptions about factors that influence success. Third, the H-DPT program was only in its second year, and it is possible that the perceptions of students would be different in a more mature, stable program. As the program matured, instructional practices became more sophisticated and consistent than they were in the first 2 years of the program. Last, the definition of "student success" was not operationally defined for the participants, because it was the authors' intentions to allow students to self-select their perception of success. This may have led to a lack of uniformity in analyzing variables impacting success.

Suggestions for future research include the following: (1) replicate the Q-sort in the H-DPT program to see if student perceptions have changed now that the program is more mature; (2) conduct a qualitative study to probe students lived experiences in the H-DPT program regarding the variables identified in this study; (3) compare student perceptions in the first versus final year of the program; (4) compare student perceptions between those students in the top versus bottom quartile measured by final grade point average.

CONCLUSION
While both hybrid and traditional students perceive time management, academic work ethic, and ability to prioritize study

focus as strongly influencing student success, self-initiation in learning, problem-solving, and organization of courses were perceived by only H-DPT students as factors influencing success whereas the instructor's ability to organize course material was only identified by the traditional DPT students. Further, there was consensus in the H-DPT cohort regarding factors influencing success compared to traditional DPT students.

REFERENCES

Akhtar-Danesh, N., Baumann, A., Kolotylo, C., Lawlor, Y., Tompkins, C., & Lee, R. (2013). Perceptions of professionalism among nursing faculty and nursing students. *Western Journal of Nursing Research, 35*(2), 248–271.

Abdulghani, H. M., Abdulmajeed, A. A., Khalil, M. S., Ahmad, F., Ponnamperuma, G. G., & Amin, Z. (2014). What factors determine academic achievement in high achieving undergraduate medical students? A qualitative study. *Medical Teacher, 36,* S43–S48.

Astin, A. W., & Antonio, A. L. (2012). *Assessment for excellence: The philosophy and practice of assessment and evaluation in higher education* (2nd ed.). Lanham, MD. Rowman & Littlefield.

Berrett, D. (2012, February 19). How "flipping" the classroom can improve the traditional lecture. *The Chronicle of Higher Education,* A16–A18.

Boucher, B., Robertson, E., Wainner, R., & Sanders B. (2013). "Flipping" Texas State University's physical therapist musculoskeletal curriculum: Implementation of a hybrid learning model. *Journal of Physical Therapy Education, 27*(3), 72–77.

Cardall, W. R., Rowan, R.C., & Bay, C. (2008). Dental education from the students' perspective: Curriculum and climate. *Journal of Dental Education, 72*(5), 600–609.

Dennis, K. E. (1986). Q-methodology: Relevance and application to nursing research. *Advances in Nursing Science, 8,* 6–17.

Garrison, D. R., & Vaughan, N. D. (2008). *Blended learning in higher education: Framework, principles, and guidelines.* San Francisco, CA: Jossey-Bass.

Kosmahl, E. M. (2005). Factors related to physical therapist license examination scores. *Journal of Physical Therapy Education, 19*(2), 52–56.

Kowalczyk, N. K. (2014). *Perceived barriers to online education by radiologic science educators. Radiologic Technology, 85*(5), 486–493.

May, W. W., Morgan, B. J., Lemke, J. C., Karst, G. M., & Stone, H. L. (1995). Model for ability-based assessment in physical therapy education. *Journal of Physical Therapy Education, 9*(1), 3–6.

Mohr, T., Ingram, D., Hayes, S., & Du, Z. (2005). Educational program characteristics and pass rates on the National Physical Therapy Examination. *Journal of Physical Therapy Education, 19*(1), 60–66.

Murray, L., McCallum, C., & Petrosino, C. (2014). Flipping the classroom experience: A comparison of online learning to traditional lecture. *Journal of Physical Therapy Education, 28*(3), 35–41.

Park, J., & Choi, H. J. (2009). Factors influencing adult learners' decision to drop or persist in online learning. *Educational Technology and Society, 12*(4), 207–214.

Portney, L. G., Watkins, M. P. (2015). *Foundations of clinical research: Applications to practice* (3rd ed.). Philadelphia, PA: F. A. Davis.

Rovai, A. P. (2003). In search of higher persistence rates in distance education online programs. *Internet and Higher Education, 6,* 1–16.

Schmolck, P. (2012). PQ Method (Version 2.33, adapted from mainframe-program Qmethod written by John Atkinson, 1992) [Computer Software]. Munich, Germany: Bundeswehr University of Munich. Retrieved from http://www.lrz-muenchen .de/~schmolck/qmethod/downpqx.htm

Schmolck, P. (2014). The PQ Method manual. Retrieved from the PQ Method website: http://schmolck.userweb.mwn.de/qmethod/ pqmanual.htm

Smith, P. J. (2005). Learning preferences and readiness for online learning. *Educational Psychology, 25*(1), 3–12.

Smith, P. J., Murphy K. L., & Mahoney, S. E. (2003). Towards identifying factors underlying readiness for online learning: An exploratory study. *Distance Education, 24*(1), 57–67.

Stott, A., & Mozer, M. (2016). Connecting learners online: Challenges and issues for nurse education—Is there a way forward? *Nurse Education Today, 39,* 152–154.

Talcott, K. S., O'Donnell, J. M., & Burns, H. K. (2013). Overcoming barriers in online workshop development: An ELITE experience. *Journal of Continuing Education in Nursing, 44*(6), 264–268.

Wong K., & Chu, D. W. K. (2014). Is the flipped classroom model effective in the perspectives of students' perceptions and benefits? In S. K. S. Cheung, J. Fong, J. Zhang, R. Kwan, & L. F. Kwok (Eds.), *Hybrid learning theory and practice, Proceedings of the 7th International Conference* (pp. 93–104). New York, NY: Springer.

Trust-Related Privacy Factors in E-Learning Environments

Susan H. Stephan

INTRODUCTION

Historically, e-learning opportunities have focused on the design and delivery of course content without significant consideration given to privacy concerns (El-Khatib, Korba, Xu, & Yee, 2003). Given the ever-increasing volume of student information that resides online, this historical lack of attention to privacy is unsustainable. As learners and instructors become more aware of the risks relating to the disclosure of student information, providers of distance education

Susan H. Stephan,
Associate Dean of Graduate and Online
Programs, NSU Shepard Broad College
of Law, 3305 College Avenue,
Fort Lauderdale, FL 33314.
E-mail: sstephan@nova.edu

courses will need more guidance in addressing these privacy risks. Today's web-based software and other tools provide the opportunity for innovation and enhanced learning environments that involve student-driven interactions (Diaz, Golas, & Gautch, 2010), but with these new tools comes a heightened privacy concern that institutions and instructors who design and implement courses online need to address.

Many factors influence student trust in an online learning environment, and privacy issues are among them (Wang, 2014). Anwar and Greer indicated that earning student trust in online learning environments is key to the success of online learning and that privacy is equally important (2012). According to Anwar and Greer (2012), "Privacy and trust are equally desirable in a learning environment. Privacy promotes safe learning, while trust promotes collaboration and healthy competition, and thereby, knowledge dissemination" (p. 62). With these propositions as a starting point, this review of the e-learning-focused privacy literature aimed to synthesize existing online educational privacy guidance available to instructors in a distance learning setting, both generally and as it related to learner trust online.

PRIVACY AND STUDENT DATA

Online tracking of individuals is becoming more common and more pervasive. Most commercial websites download some form of tracking software onto users' computers, from cookies that store user names and passwords to perhaps hundreds of files or programs, most of which typically originate from companies that track and sell web user data (Angwin, 2010). The presence of tracking programs is not always apparent to an Internet user. These programs often come from hidden files within downloads or display ads. Certainly, consumers might appreciate the personalized experience that is made possible through a third party comprehensively tracking Internet behavior, but relevant, targeted ads are just one result of online data collection. This type of data that is "mined" from a user's online activity is a significant source of revenue for web-based companies, and it stands to gain in net worth as more interested parties discover the value of collected information and are willing to pay for it.

It follows that from a business standpoint, it is valuable to know as much as possible about a consumer and what he or she typically is seeking. As technology progresses, the process of researching consumer behavior is becoming increasingly accurate and efficient in every way, and the level of sophistication of tracking technologies continues to rise. To the extent that an online learner is situated similarly to an online consumer of noneducational goods or services, the value of an online student's mined data can be just as high. Therefore, concerns with privacy and student data security are real.

Government agencies worldwide have adopted privacy laws and policies aimed at protecting personal information (El-Khatib et al., 2003). In the United States, a public interest in educational privacy is reflected by several laws that aim to protect student privacy, including Family Educational Rights and Privacy Act of 1974 (FERPA) and the Higher Education Opportunity Act (2008), as well as the Children's Online Privacy Protection Act (1998) as it relates to collecting personal information from per-

sons under the age of 13, and of course broader privacy regulation including the Privacy Act of 1974; the proposed Consumer Privacy Protection Act (2015); recent state legislation in Illinois (the Illinois Biometric Information Privacy Act); Texas (the Capture or Use of Biometric Identifier), aimed specifically at the use of biometrics in online settings; Washington's biometric identifier law which became effective on July 23, 2017; and California's Student Online Personal Information Protection Act, which went into effect in January of 2016 and addresses personal information on websites, applications and online services that focus on K–12 students. A comprehensive survey of laws and their application to the e-learning environment is outside the scope of this review but would prove informative to future research and literature addressing privacy. The main goal of this review is to identify existing literature that addresses FERPA and other privacy concerns in e-learning environments and to then consider a framework for future exploration through literature of the challenges of online educational privacy issues, including those issues that specifically relate to learner trust.

FERPA (20 U.S.C. § 1232g; 34 CFR Part 99) (1974), a Federal law that protects the privacy of student education records, is at the forefront of student privacy concerns and applies to all schools that receive funds under an applicable program of the U.S. Department of Education. Going forward, the interpretation of FERPA and its applicability to online course design and implementation will necessarily inform the use of online tools in support of distance education as a starting point for establishing privacy best practices (Diaz et al., 2010). For example, when adopting a course management system platform as well as collaborative technologies such as social media, blogs and wikis, and screencasting tools, an instructor is asking course participants to share with service providers a variety of information, some of which learners will consider private (Kim, 2013).

Generally, institution-licensed course management system platforms such as Blackboard have a privacy policy that invokes FERPA and discloses that the company collects personally identifiable information from or about students. Blackboard's Privacy Policy stated that it considers student data to be "strictly confidential and in general does not use it for any purpose other than improving and providing our Services to the school or on the school's behalf." (sec. 7, para. 1). The policy also purports to comply with the U.S.-EU Safe Harbor Framework and the U.S.-Swiss Safe Harbor Framework as set forth by the U.S. Department of Commerce regarding the collection, use, and retention of personal information from European Union member countries and Switzerland. In comparison, free and open source course management system platforms that do not offer an educational license generally say nothing about FERPA and do not purport to comply with data protection laws from jurisdictions outside the United States. In other words, social media and other free software and applications potentially open the academic environment to the public (Rodriguez, 2011).

Despite this increased likelihood of exposure of student data through online distance education courses, there is an apparent gap in literature that speaks to this topic. This review examined literature that provided a starting point to the student privacy discourse.

LITERATURE REVIEW

Asllani (2012) discussed FERPA requirements in the context of online education but focused on student information, including financial data, records, advising opportunities, and grades as opposed to course content. Almost 10 years ago, Alexander, Jones and Brown (1998) also addressed privacy concerns of faculty and students regarding the potential compromise of private data, but this survey was not aimed at online education; rather, it addressed the educational information that institutions store digitally. Similarly, Culnan and Carlin (2008) discussed educational privacy concerns related to data breach and theft of information such as social security numbers and alumni data, as opposed to data related to online coursework.

Daries et al. (2014) focused on FERPA regulations and distance education in the context of massive open online courses (MOOCs). However, Daries et al. (2014) discussed the intentional release of de-identified student data in order to promote research on the composition of MOOC-enrolled students and to add to the body of literature about MOOCs. FERPA, in this situation, according to the authors, was a hindrance to social science research because of privacy concerns. Interestingly, Daries et al. (2014) also noted, "not all institutions consider MOOC learners to be subject to FERPA" (p. 58). This might come into play as social scientists continue to work toward future data releases.

With similar goals for the use of student data, Goyal and Vohra (2012) supported the mining of students' educational data, or educational datamining, in various settings. They proposed that datamining in higher education could help to improve student performance, learning outcomes, course choices, and retention through the collection, analysis, interpretation, and presentation of educational datamining (Goyal & Vohra, 2012). Goyal and Vohra (2012) described the two primary student data collection methods in an e-learning environment as (a) statistics—or the review of files and databases to determine information such as where students enter an exit the online environment, the most popular web pages, the number of resource downloads, pages actually browsed by a student, and the time the student spent on a page; and (b) visualization—looking at patterns of student users' online behavior and data such as summative assessment scores, tracked attendance and group activity. Goyal and Vohra (2012) did not explicitly discuss the privacy implications of educational datamining, but they did address data security of warehousing the mined student data. Of course, many of the privacy concerns that FERPA attempts to address, and that scholars possibly implicate with their proposed mining and use of student data, might also be the basis of issues with learner trust in an online education environment. But a review of the literature in this sub-area of online educational privacy concerns leads to limited consideration and discourse related to a framework for examining issues of privacy-related trust in distance learning environments.

There is a significant body of literature that has addressed the importance of building trust in distance learning environments (e.g., Brookfield, 2015; Carchiolo, Correnti, Longheu, Malgeri, & Mangioni, 2008; Liu, Chen, & Sun, 2011; Wang, 2014). A search for literature that has taken into account the trust-related privacy implications of e-learning environments resulted in a much smaller dataset. Wang (2014) was one of the few scholars who framed a discussion of participant trust in online education communities against a privacy backdrop; she proposed a "social-technical framework of trust-inducing factors" (p. 347) in distance education, which discussed privacy and security issues based on approaches found in the literature of El-Khatib et al. (2003) and Anwar and Greer (2012). Wang (2014) classified 12 features of trusted learning environments into four groups: (a) credibility, (b) design, (c) instructor sociocommunicative style, and (d) privacy and security. Wang (2014) suggested that important aspects of a framework of trust-inducing factors for online educators are: posting a clear and sufficient privacy policy, using security measures in design and access to distance

learning environments, and complying with accepted U.S. and E.U. security standards.

El-Khatib et al. (2003) discussed privacy principles in Canada as they related to various learning technology standards, specifically addressing "trust mechanisms" between learning platform users and service providers. They proposed that the service providers need to trust that a learner is actually the individual authorized to take a particular course, and that the learners need to trust the service that is provided. More accurately, according to El-Khatib et al. (2003), "the learner must believe the service provider will only use his/her private information, such as a name, address, credit card details, preferences, and learning behavior in a manner expressed in the policy provided for the e-learning system user" (p. 14). El-Khatib et al. (2003), presented the infrastructure for the framework of the digital authentication of provider trust, and provided a technical overview of trust management systems. This direction approached learner trust from the technology instead of the privacy regulation perspective and did not provide practical guidance at the instructor level.

Anwar and Greer (2012) also addressed trust in e-learning environments, focusing on trust relationships among co-learners, through identity management models for e-learning forums. Through a privacy-enhancing identity management model, Anwar and Greer (2012) proposed a pseudonymous "partial identity" for online collaborators to determine an effective reputation management system that would allow learners to present themselves anonymously. As with the El-Khatib et al. (2003) modeling, the Anwar and Greer (2012) insights, although they presented an interesting perspective on co-learner trust, did not provide instructor-level guidance.

Finally, Diaz (2010) suggested that to foster trust when using a publically available facilitating technology or service provider, an instructor should include a statement in the course syllabus that confirms that the student consents to the use of specific collaborative tools that are open to the public and that the contributions to the tool might be part of the student's educational record that will be disclosed. Tang, Hu, and Smith (2008) ostensibly supported Diaz (2010) when they indicated that privacy protection measures, such as privacy policies, can enhance levels of consumer trust and are likely effective in terms of consumers online; however, they also pointed out that the costs of increased privacy measures might create inefficiencies that have negative effects on social welfare. This concept translates well to online learning environments, although the authors did not specifically address education in their consumer-based analyses.

It is worth considering that the increased cost and time commitment of heightened privacy measures—from drafting new privacy policies to researching platforms, to monitoring third-party data collection and use—might be unattractive to institutions, faculty, and students. This might be an explanation for the lack of a push to add educational privacy standards and measures more quickly, and it also might explain the relatively small body of literature supporting research and standards related to e-learning privacy issues. Whatever the reason, there is a dearth of literature providing helpful insights into FERPA, trust-related privacy concerns, and other privacy and data security risks in e-learning environments.

CONCLUSION

Technology does not stand still. The dynamic evolution of distance education continues to incorporate the latest technological advances on its quest to reach more and more learners across the globe. There was a time when writing was a new technology; today, educators can collaborate with learners through real time idea-sharing written discourse, audio-visual discussion threads, and videoconferencing; track learners' movements, patterns and activity within an online learning platform; and facilitate online tests that are proctored via biometric identity authentication. Educational relationships online take data sharing to a whole new level, on a variety of platforms and devices. But what, exactly, are participants in the average learning environment sharing—and do they know? As applied to distance education, privacy laws are nascent and hardly able to keep up with the evolving technologies that instructors and students employ. Additional research is needed to support a framework within which to address privacy under FERPA and other privacy regulations—and to contribute to an environment of trust—in online distance courses and communities.

REFERENCES

Alexander, P., Jones, T. M., & Brown, S. (n.d.). AIS Electronic Library (AISeL). Retrieved from http://aisel.aisnet.org/amcis1998/17/

Angwin, J. (2010, July 10). The web's new goldmine: Your secrets. Retrieved from http://www.wsj.com/articles/SB10001424052748703940904575395073512989404

Anwar, M., & Greer, J. (2012). Facilitating trust in privacy-preserving e-learning environments. *IEEE Transactions on Learning Technologies, 5*(1), 62–73.

Asllani, A. (2012, February). Privacy concerns in higher education traditional versus online education. *International Journal of Computer Science and Information Security, 10*(2), 6–10.

Biometric Indentifiers Act, Washington Laws of 2017, ch. 299 § 1 (2017).

Biometric Information Privacy Act, 740 ILCS 14 (2008).

Blackboard. (n.d.). Blackboard Privacy Policy. Retrieved from http://www.blackboard.com/footer/privacy-policy.aspx

Brookfield, S. (2015). What students value in teachers. In *The skillful teacher: On technique, trust, and responsiveness in the classroom* (3rd, ed., pp. 41–55). San Francisco, CA: Jossey-Bass.

Children's Online Privacy Protection Act of 1998, 15 U.S.C. §§ 6501-6505 (1998).

Capture or Use of Biometric Identifier Act, Tex. Bus. & Com. Code Ann. § 503.001 (2009).

Consumer Privacy Protection Act, S. 1158, 114th Cong. (2015).

Carchiolo, V., Correnti, D., Longheu, A., Malgeri, M., & Mangioni, G. (n.d.). Reliable personalized learning paths: The contribution of trust to e-learning. In V. Carchiolo (Ed.), *The Open Knowledge Society: A computer science and information systems manifesto* (pp. 221–228). Retrieved from http://www.academia .edu/4992485/Reliable_Personalized_ Learning_Paths_The_Contribution_of_ Trust_to_E-Learning

Culnan, M. J., & Carlin, T. J. (2009). Online privacy practices in higher education: Making the grade? *Communications of the ACM, 52*(3), 126–130. Retrieved from http://cacm.acm .org/magazines/2009/3/21796-online-privacy-practices-in-higher-education/fulltext

Daries, J. P., Reich, J., Waldo, J., Young, E. M., Whittinghill, J., Ho, A. D., ... Chuang, I. (2014). Privacy, anonymity, and big data in the social sciences. *Communications of the ACM, 57*(9), 56–63. doi:10.1145/2643132

Diaz, V. (2010). Web 2.0 and emerging technologies in online learning. *New Directions for Community Colleges, 2010*(150), 57–66. doi:10.1002/cc.405

Diaz, V., Golas, J., & Gautch, S. (2010). Computer-based learning environments. *SpringerReference*. doi:10.1007/ springerreference_302375

El-Khatib, K., Korba, L., Xu, Y., & Yee, G. (2003). Privacy and security in e-learning. *International Journal of Distance Education Technologies, 1*(4), 1–19. doi:10.4018/jdet.2003100101

Family Educational Rights and Privacy Act of 1974, 20 U.S.C. § 1232g *et seq.* (1974).

Goyal, M., Vohra, R. (March 2012). Applications of data mining in higher education. *International Journal of Computer Science Issues, 9*(2), 113–120.

Higher Education Opportunity Act, P.L. 110-115 (2008).

Kim, H. (2013). E-learning privacy and security requirements: Review. *JSE Journal of Security Engineering, 10*(5), 591–600. doi:10.14257/ jse.2013.10.5.07

Liu, Y., Chen, D., & Sun, J. (2011). *Proceedings of 2011 International Conference on Web Information Systems and Mining.* Retrieved from http://www.researchgate.net/publication/ 252008188_A_trustworthy_e-learning_ based_on_trust_and_quality_evaluation

Privacy Act of 1974, P.L. 93–579, 88 Stat. 1896, enacted December 31, 1974, 5 U.S.C. § 552a (1974).

Rodriguez, J. E. (2011). Social media use in higher education: Key areas to consider for educators. *Merlot Journal of Online Learning and Teaching, 7*(4), 539–550.

Tang, Z., Hu, Y., & Smith, M. D. (2008). Gaining trust through online privacy protection: self-regulation, mandatory standards, or *caveat emptor. Journal of Management Information Systems, 24*(4), 153–173. doi:10.2753/mis0742-1222240406

Wang, Y. D. (2014). Building student trust in online learning environments. *Distance Education, 35*(3), 345–359. doi:10.1080/01587919 .2015.955267

Is Technology Only a Vehicle?

Christopher Voltmer

INTRODUCTION

Teaching is an art that is defined as "providing instruction" and "imparting knowledge," as per Merriam Webster (Merriam-Webster, n.d.). Teaching can occur in a myriad of arenas and through different methods. Is it possible that one delivery method for teaching could be superior to another? In 1983, Richard Clark began a controversial debate regarding the use of various media sources for education purposes. Clark stated,

> The best current evidence is that media are mere vehicles that deliver instruction but do not influence student achievement

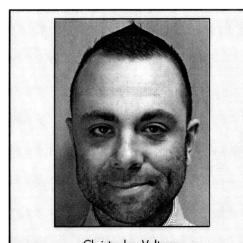

Christopher Voltmer,
Touro College, 1700 Union Boulevard,
Bay Shore, NY 11706.
Telephone: (631) 665-1600, ext. 6235.
E-mail: christopher.voltmer@touro.edu

any more than the truck that delivers groceries causes changes in our nutrition. Basically, the choice of vehicle might influence the cost or extent of distributing instruction, but only the content of the vehicle can influence achievement. (Clark, 1983, p. 445)

Clark's argument is that media technology, by itself, will not influence learning. Learning will occur more through some aspect of educational design and instructional methodology.

THE BACKGROUND

Educators strive to create the perfect learning environment and experience for those individuals who are being taught. Technological advances within media are continually occurring and therefore it should not come as a shock that this evolution is being utilized more for teaching. Does this mean that media will become a better source of education and teaching? Should all the other methods be thought of as outdated? Clark has not believed this to be the case for nearly 35 years! It is Clark's stance that media should not replace the value placed on creating strong instructional methods. In 1994, he described instructional methods as being able to stimulate the cognitive processes necessary for learning and motivation (Clark, 1994).

It is through instructional methods that a learner will become aware of what is expected from an educational experience. In *Health Professional as Educator: Principles of Teaching and Learning*, Kathleen Fitzgerald describes the advantages and disadvantages of many different types of instructional methods. These include but are not limited to: lecture, group instruction, one-to-one instruction, demonstration, return demonstration, gaming, simulation, role-playing, role modeling, and self-instruction. Several factors should be considered when deciding which method to utilize. These include the characteristics of the audience, experience of the educator, objectives of a learning experience, the cost effectiveness, and the setting learning is to occur (Fitzgerald, 2011). It is Clark's belief that correctly selecting an appropriate instructional method is the key. He is not stating that media and all its wonderful achievements and advancements cannot be an excellent tool for learning but that media without proper design is useless.

Kozma has been an opponent of Clark's "mere vehicles" stance. It is Kozma's belief that learning is extremely dependent on media as a medium for transmission of information necessary for learning to occur (Kozma, 1994). A strong stance is taken that it is nearly impossible to separate the two. Kozma does seem to agree with Clark that there needs to be solid instructional methods and designs for learning to occur. The problem with Kozma's argument is that it needed to be supported more by evidence.

ACADEMIC SETTING

The academic world is continually changing. More pressure has been put on physical therapists to earn advanced degrees. There are more clinical professionals that have decided to receive transitional doctorates in physical therapy and PhD degrees in related fields. State regulations are continually changing which are forcing certain continuing education credits to maintain licensure. With the wide variety of media options available it has made receiving this education easier but not necessarily better. It must be evaluated which

media options are appropriate and can be accessed and used to the advantage of all students. To properly create an educational experience that is worthwhile, educational design and structure must be utilized. It is possible that a mixture of different delivery mediums may be the most advantageous for students. As originally proposed by Hastings and Tracey it might be time to start a new study and debate regarding how media affects learning, and not if media affects learning (Hastings & Tracey, 2005).

CLINICAL SETTING

Clinically, physical therapists are continually educating and teaching our patients. A physical therapist may teach a patient a home exercise program to strengthen a weak muscle or educate someone on a more efficient resting posture. All patients deserve access to the highest quality care. In the past half century, it has been brought to attention that many people living in remote towns and cities do not receive access to the same quality health care as those living in large cities. One possible and cost-effective solution to this issue is telehealth. Telehealth, often referred to as telemedicine, is broadly defined as a means to provide different health related services and information utilizing various communication technologies at a distance (Lee, 2012). Although telehealth is not new, advancements in technology have made telecommunication materials more available. Telehealth has proven to be efficient for both patients and health care providers.

There are two types of telehealth: real time and store-and-forward applications. When using real-time telehealth, an individual can send information instantly with little delay. Examples of real-time telehealth are a telephone call and a videoconference. Benefits of real-time telehealth are that decisions can be made immediately, and if a clinician needs information, they can request it immediately. Store-and-forward applications are created when information is created and then transmitted to the recipient for a response at a different time (Smith, Bensink, Armfield, Stillman, & Cattery, 2005). Examples of this would be an e-mail or fax. The benefit of this type of telehealth is that individuals can examine material at a time that is most convenient for them. When deciding which form of telehealth to use, the consumer must keep in mind how fast they need a reply and what type of information needs to be sent.

When referring to physical therapy practice in the arena of telehealth it is only appropriate to call it telerehabilitation. Physical therapists cannot keep this word all to themselves, as it also encompasses occupational therapists, speech therapists, and other members involved in a rehabilitation team. If you were to talk to an individual with an eye in the past, the word telerehabilitation may seem far too futuristic. The truth is the future is now. The term includes a large range of services that include "assessment, monitoring, prevention, intervention, supervision, education, consultation, and counseling" (Brennan, 2010, p. 31). Services can often be received at many different locations including health care settings, clinics, homes, schools, and other community locations.

CONSIDERATIONS

As one can imagine, there are quite a few issues and concerns when it comes to media as a form of education and teaching. Connection issues due to bandwidth and telephone service pose as a major threat. Natural disasters can also be an issue because telephone poles and cable lines can be destroyed. These issues, along with the possibility of software and hardware failure would prevent the health care provider from being able to provide services for clinical and educational purposes. Students learning for courses for a collegiate degree, post professional courses, or con-

tinuing education would be affected as well. When it comes to telehealth there must be a patient and clinician acceptance of decreased interaction between one another. Some people reveal feeling safer in a hospital setting with a clinician present, compared to their own homes without a healthcare professional there (Eron, 2010). Other items to be aware of when deciding whether media technology is appropriate would be the learners fear of something new, the cost effectiveness of the form of media utilized, and being certain to choose the appropriate type of media.

CONCLUSION

Although decades old, Clark's original stance caries significant substance today. In recent years media technology has progressed to a point where life is unrecognizable without it. In certain instances, it has allowed individuals to receive degrees that would have never been possible without the use of media. It must be remembered that although this media is great, it cannot replace the hard work that must be put into creating a successful educational experience. Content, organization, care and enthusiasm, and the willingness to learn must always be evaluated.

REFERENCES

Brennan D., Tindall, L., & Theodoros, D. (2010). A blueprint for telerehabilitation guidelines. *International Journal of Telemedicine Applications, 2*(2), 31–34. doi:10.5195ijt.2010.6063

Clark, R. E. (1983). Reconsidering research on learning from media. *Review of Educational Research, 53*(4), 445–449.

Clark, R. E. (1994). Media will never influence learning. *Educational Technology Research and Development, 42*(2), 21–29.

Eron, L. (2010). Telemedicine: The future of outpatient therapy? *Clinical Infectious Diseases, 51*, S224–S230. doi:10.1086/653524

Fitzgerald, K. (2011). Instructional methods and settings. In S. B. Bastable, P. Gramet, K. Jacobs, & D. L. Sopszyk (Eds.), *Health profes-*

sional as educator: Principles of teaching and learning (pp. 421–462). Sudbury, MA: Jones & Bartlett.

Hastings, N. B., & Tracey, M. W. (2005). Does media affect learning: Where are we now? *Tech Trends, 49*(2), 28–30.

Kozma, R. B. (1994). Will media influence learning: Reframing the debate. *Educational Technology Research and Development, 42*(2), 7–19.

Lee, A. C., & Harada, N. D. (2012). Telehealth as a Means of Health Care Delivery. *Physical Therapy, 92,* 463–468.

Merriam-Webster. (n.d.) Teaching. Retrieved from http://www.merriam-webster.com/dictionary/teaching

Smith, A. C., Bensink, M. M., Armfield, N. N., Stillman, J. J., & Cattery, L. (2005). Telemedicine and rural health care applications. *Journal of Postgraduate Medicine, 51*(4), 286–293.

Some "Must-Read" Reports About the State of Online Education

Natalie B. Milman

There are several reports published annually about online education in higher and K–12 education that I read every year, and that list is growing. I read these not only to keep up with the field, but also to learn about innovations and trends that I should be researching and/or incorporating into my courses. My

Natalie B. Milman,
Associate Professor,
Graduate School of Education and Human
Development, The George Washington
University, 2134 G ST, NW, Washington, DC
20052. Telephone: (202) 994-1884.
E-mail: nmilman@gwu.edu

"must read" list now also includes the *Changing Landscape of Online Education* by Legon and Garrett (2017), underwritten by Quality Matters and Eduventures. The authors of this report conducted a survey of "chief online officers at community colleges, four-year public, and 4-year private, nonprofit colleges and universities" (p. 5). This survey, to be administered annually, provides baseline data from chief online officers, the individuals within these institutions who manage online education. As online education changes, it will be important to learn about decisions and trends from their perspectives.

The findings of the CHLOE report provide a snapshot of online education from the chief online officer's point of view. It is a unique perspective in that individuals in such positions are viewed as key decision-makers of online education in community colleges and universities. As Legon and Garrett (2017) noted, "At many institutions, management of online-related activities and responsibilities ... [are] consolidated under the leadership of a single institutional officer" (p. 5). Therefore, surveying this group annually can potentially provide an important view of the community college and 4-year university online education landscape, as well as help substantiate

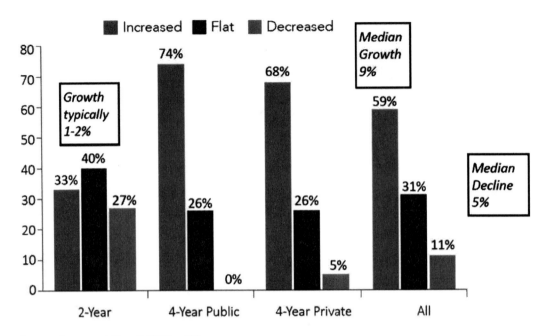

Source: Legon and Garrett (2017, p. 13).

Figure 1. Fully online student headcount growth from spring 2015 to 2016.

findings from other reports examining online education from different stakeholders. For example, of 104 usable surveys, Figure 1 shows student headcounts from spring 2015 to 2016 increased, particularly in 4-year public and private universities.

These findings are consistent with findings from other reports, such as the more recent report sponsored by the Online Learning Consortium by Seaman, Allen, and Seaman (2018), where the authors also discovered "The number of distance education students grew by 5.6% from fall 2015 to fall 2016 to reach 6,359,121 who are taking at least one distance course, representing 31.6% of all students" (p. 3).

Other reports that help keep me informed about online education and technology innovation include, but are not limited to the:

- International Association for K–12 Online Learning's, or iNACOL (see https://www.inacol.org/resources/

resource-search/?resource_types=20): iNACOL publishes several reports each year. Of the reports iNACOL publishes, I make it a point to read those in the *Keeping Pace* series. These reports examine K–12 online and often also blended education. The focus of the report varies year-to-year; even so, it is a highly recommended addition to your list of must-reads even if you do not teach or work in K–12 education. Seeing what is coming up in the pipeline can certainly influence those of us in higher education!

- Online Learning Consortium annual surveys of academic leaders of online learning, previously known as the Sloan Surveys (see https://secure.onlinelearningconsortium.org/publications/surveys): now in its 10th year, these reports provide definitions of distance education and data about online student enrollments in institutions of higher education.

- NMC *Horizon Reports* (see https:// www.nmc.org/nmc-horizon/): These were well-known reports examining key technology trends in higher education, K–12 education, libraries, and museums; however, the organization filed for bankruptcy last year (Lederman, 2017) so the future of these reports continuing is uncertain.

Other groups publish reports, as well, that are worth reading; see for example:

- Accenture's *Technology Vision 2017*: https://www.accenture.com/us-en/ insight-disruptive-technology-trends-2017
- Deloitte's *Tech Trends 2018*: https:// www2.deloitte.com/insights/us/en/ focus/tech-trends.html
- Gartner's *Top 10 Strategic Technology Trends for 2018*: https://www.gartner .com/smarterwithgartner/gartner-top-10-strategic-technology-trends-for-2018/

Keeping informed in an ever-changing field is important. These are just a few of the many reports that I recommend reading for those involved in online higher education.

REFERENCES

Lederman, D. (2017, December 20). New Media Consortium suddenly folds [Blog post]. Retrieved from https://www.insidehighered .com/quicktakes/2017/12/20/new-media-consortium-suddenly-folds

Legon, R., & Garrett, R. (2017). *Changing landscape of online education (CHLOE): Quality Matters & Eduventures survey of chief online officers.* Retrieved from https://www.quality-matters.org/sites/default/files/research-docs-pdfs/CHLOE-First-Survey-Report.pdf

Seaman, J. E., Allen, I. E., & Seaman, J. (2018). *Grade increase tracking distance education in the United States.* Retrieved from https://secure .onlinelearningconsortium.org/node/384451

PROGRAMS AND DEGREES

UNDERGRADUATE
BACHELOR'S DEGREES
Cardiovascular Sonography (B.S.)*, Fort Lauderdale/Davie Campus
Exercise and Sport Science (B.S.), Fort Lauderdale/Davie Campus
Health Science (B.H.Sc.)**
Medical Sonography (B.S.), Fort Lauderdale/Davie Campus
Respiratory Therapy (B.S.), Palm Beach Campus
Respiratory Therapy (B.S.)**
Speech Language and Communication Disorders (B.S.), Fort Lauderdale/Davie Campus

GRADUATE
MASTER'S DEGREES
Anesthesia (M.S.), Fort Lauderdale/Davie Campus
Anesthesia (M.S.), Tampa Campus
Health Science (M.H.Sc.)**
Occupational Therapy (M.O.T.), Fort Lauderdale/Davie Campus
Physician Assistant (M.M.S.), Fort Lauderdale/Davie Campus
Physician Assistant (M.M.S.), Fort Myers Campus
Physician Assistant (M.M.S.), Jacksonville Campus
Physician Assistant (M.M.S.), Orlando Campus
Speech-Language Pathology (M.S.)‡, Fort Lauderdale/Davie Campus

DOCTORAL DEGREES
Audiology (Au.D.), Fort Lauderdale/Davie Campus
Audiology (Au.D.), United Kingdom
Health Science (D.H.Sc.)**
Health Science (Ph.D.)**
Occupational Therapy (O.T.D.)‡, Tampa Campus
Occupational Therapy (Dr.O.T.)**
Occupational Therapy (Ph.D.)**
Physical Therapy (D.P.T.), Fort Lauderdale/Davie Campus
Physical Therapy (D.P.T.)‡, Tampa Campus
Physical Therapy (D.P.T., transition)**
Physical Therapy (Ph.D.)**
Speech-Language Pathology (SLP.D.)**

healthsciences.nova.edu

*A dual degree B.S. Cardiovascular Sonography/M.H.Sc. program is available at the NSU Tampa Campus.
**Programs are available either completely or partially online.
‡Programs are offered in a hybrid format that combines online and on-campus elements.

New Look to an Old Course? No Need to Panic!

Errol Craig Sull

I t is always comfortable and relaxing for the online educator: starting another session, another quarter, another semester with the same online course you've previously taught—and the course looks and feels the same! Oh, sure, there may have been a tweak here or a trim there, but overall it is an old friend; the course you just finished teaching. But

Errol Craig Sull,
Adjunct Professor, Department of English,
Drexel University, P.O. Box 956,
Buffalo, NY 14207.
Telephone: (716) 871-1900.
E-mail: erroldistancelearning@gmail.com

then it happens: you learn your course will be fully redesigned and revised—not only a new look but also new content. Oh, no! This can be stressful, unnerving, and dispiriting, but it does not have to be. In fact, it can be refreshing and invigorating—and a wonderful opportunity! Here's how:

- **Read all materials on new course structure—and save it:** You will be receiving e-mails and other info relating to the course revision/redesign. Of course, read all that comes your way, but also save each item in a "New Course" folder on your computer. But just saving it without using it won't do you much good—be sure you read it over (more than once!) ... and compare the changes described to your present course. This latter suggestion is important; it gives you the opportunity to begin getting used to the new course and to outline changes you intend on making to your teaching the course. There are great opportunities here for new or expanded teaching strategies and materials!
- **Attend all training for the revised course —#1:** This is a given, but something that is easy to miss (unless it is required). Nearly all online schools

offering new versions of an old course will hold webinars for faculty to discuss the nuances—big and small—of the revised course. Not only will valuable information be offered, but you also have the opportunity to ask questions and get clarification in live time. Keep in mind that, no matter how thorough the information and training for a revised course may be, there will always be additional questions asked or clarification needed simply because each person has a different approach to teaching.

- **Attend all training for the revised course—#2:** Being active in the training is important, and this can be summed up in three actions: (1) ask questions when you need more info—and be sure to listen and/or view what your colleagues offer: there will be valuable information that will only enhance your smooth teaching of the new course; (2) download any items that are made available relating to the reconfigured course; (3) take notes: no doubt the presentation will be recorded and archived for later view, but rather than going through the entire webinar again, taking notes on what is most important to you will save time. (Certainly, visit the recording if you are unsure of any note you took!)

- **Thoroughly explore the course prior to students having access:** No matter how much information and training you are given for a new course, nothing gives you a better sense of your course than "hands-on" exploration of it. First, take a tour in every nook and cranny of the course (as you do, ask yourself, "What questions might my students have on the course layout, assignments, etc.?")—you want to become as familiar with the course as a tour guide would of a city! (And although your school might require you to submit a checklist of items required to set up your course, again, this is a checklist—not an intimate stroll through the streets of your

course!) And if you find an area where you might need a bit more of a reminder, make a note to keep yourself on track.

- **Make note of any errors, oversights, vagueness, and "confusions":** The first release of a reconfigured course is akin to the release of a first edition software: it is Revised Course 1.0. And just as software releases patches and updated versions to correct errors and oversights, so, too, will future "editions" of your course no doubt correct oversights and errors, as well as items that need clarification. Take notes on anything you believe could be improved—the folks in charge of the revision will welcome these, as what is ultimately important is a smooth, enjoyable, and substantive course for the students. A first edition of a new course is always a rough edition—help it strive toward perfection!

- **Use reminder software or a notepad to keep track of important dates:** Online education has a variety of important dates all faculty must know: when faculty postings are to be made, the dates for student e-mails and reminders, due dates for assignments, and others. With a revised course these may have changed, and you don't want to miss any, so use reminder software (memotome.com is a great one—and it's free) or a schedule pad to be sure you don't miss any "must" days to do this or that. And don't just stop with "this has to be done"—include those additional postings and other items that you want to do to help the students' experience. Relying fully on your mind will inevitably result in some dates missed—something you never want.

- **Anticipate what materials students will need for assignments—not day by day:** It can seem much easier to post materials and announcements and emails to students as a new week arrives—yet doing this "now" approach to teaching a new course can have negative results for students and you. As an example: if you are teaching an English course, and the students must begin using research including references in a Week 3 essay, do not wait until Week 3 to give them information on how to correctly use citations (in-text and references or works cited page), but rather introduce it in Week 1 so students have time to get used to it, to experiment with it. Teaching "by the seat of your pants" can take away from students' learning, from their willingness to submit assignments (they might be intimidated or downright scared of this new learning creature!), and from your overall effectiveness in the classroom. So when looking over your course before students arrive decide what you can offer them ahead of certain assignments to better prepare them for the assignments.

- **Offer additional materials as are allowed:** No course can be fully inclusive in the materials that have been included in that course. Why? Each student is different, each faculty member is different, and these equate to enhancements of or additions to materials that come with the revised course. Depending on the course set-up and school guidelines, additional materials from faculty can be added attachments in the course, attachments to student e-mails, information in e-mails and announcements, minivideos, live chats, and/or other items. Go with the flow; use the possibilities that do exist for giving students added materials, and when you do always make those materials the kind that will do the most good for the most amount of students. (If one or two students are having repeated difficulty with understanding what caused the Civil War, for example, it would probably be more beneficial to write and/or call each student with more clarification.)

- **Do ongoing outreach to your students to help eliminate confusion:** Outreach to students is always important, but this becomes especially crucial with a revised and redesigned course. Although some students may not have been used to another course design, the course should be approached as a new one, even if but one student had an older design/format of the course. And if all students are used to this course redesign (because it appeared in previous courses they took) still do extensive outreach: as this is Revised Course 1.0 there might be vagueness, inconsistencies, incorrect info, or disconnects (that will no doubt be corrected in Revised Course 2.0)—and you want to be sure students are as informed and "unconfused" as possible. And don't forget: where your school allows it, also make outreach phone calls; this is a personal contact that can have much better results than e-mails or texts.

- **Stay in contact with your supervisor:** There are many reasons for staying in touch with your supervisor when a revised course is launched: let the person know of any "oops!" you discover in the new course; offer suggestions that might make Revised Course 2.0 a bit smoother and less confusing; if you want to add something to the course but are unsure if you are allowed to do so—ask; for any information you receive on the course revision or redesign but are unsure of any part of the info, touch base with your supervisor for clarification. You always want to give the impression of having your supervisor in the know about any new items you intend on including in the revised course ... and to ask for any clarification so you don't guess ... wrongly!

- **Makes notes on additional problems encountered/suggestions for improvement while the course is live:** Only once your course is "live," with students wandering about and assignments coming due, will you chance upon new problems, difficulties, or confusion in the shape of vague wording, items mentioned but left out of the course, disconnects in assignments, et cetera. that were not discovered while the course was in a "ready" state. Keep an ongoing list of these, and as soon as one appears—and you are positive it has not already been addressed—let your supervisor know. You are a main cog in helping Revised Course 2.0 become a version of the course that is easier, more enjoyable, and more effective than Revised Course 1.0!

Remember: When a restaurant changes its menu, we adapt. When a TV show loses our favorite character, we adapt. When a football team returns with a new roster, we adapt. That's what we do!

Ask Errol!

Errol Craig Sull

D istance learning has certainly come a long way since its beginning many years ago, but the challenges and difficulties that new technology, new approaches to education, and more complex online learning platforms bring equate to ongoing questions and confusion from distance educators. And that's why I write my columns: to help you with a bit more clarification, some new suggestions, and updated information. I

Errol Craig Sull,
Adjunct Professor, Department of English,
Drexel University, P.O. Box 956,
Buffalo, NY 14207.
Telephone: (716) 871-1900.
E-mail: erroldistancelearning@gmail.com

look forward to your e-mails in the coming year, and responding.

Some excellent questions:

It's been a long year for me, Errol, and I speak here of distance learning. I'm rather new to teaching online, and in each of my classes I've had students who previously failed the same course. This I did not expect, and I find that I'm teaching, in essence, two different kinds of students, and I fear I'm not giving the repeating students the kind of assistance they really need. (By the way: if I compare their passing rates to students taking the course for the first time there is a stark difference: 27% versus 71% for the nonrepeating students.) I teach American History, and any help you can give me would be appreciated.

Ah, are you asking the right person this question! About a year ago I decided these repeating students—I'll call them "R" students—were not getting the focus they needed, so I requested one of my classes be made up of 100% "R" students. This has made a huge difference, and while I'm not suggesting you do that, there are a few things I've learned that can help. First, outreach is crucial—via e-mail, to be sure, but if your school allows it, also by phone call. And ask each student why he or she had trouble with the course previously; many will tell you why, and often you'll get information that can better help students in your current course. Also, the constant outreach shows you care; letting students know you are always there to help them is crucial. Another important aid for these students: create a step-by-step guide to completing each assignment, ending by showing what an assignment should resemble. All students in your course will benefit from this, but especially the "R" students; many times, they get confused by or need more clarification on assignment directions. Finally, as you see any of these students faltering in class—either not turning in assignments or doing very poorly on assignments—be sure to reach out to them, reminding them of their goal for a degree and the importance of your course in the professional world. Do these suggestions, and I know your passing percentages for "R" students will increase!

Errol, your tips and insights on teaching online have been really helpful over the years. As this year comes to an end I wanted to thank you, and tell you how much I look forward to your columns in the coming year. And it is the coming year that has me asking you for help! Although I've been teaching online for several years, it is a part-time endeavor for me; I do have a full-time job (in the area of accounting). Recently, I received a big promotion, and this will entail visiting some of our accounts in Europe, Australia, and Latin America. I enjoy teaching online, but, of course, my full-time position must take priority. What do you suggest about my teaching out of the United States?

First, thanks so much for the positive feedback—it's nice to know my efforts are helping folks! Distance learning is fun, but it also offers many challenges, and I always hope my experience in the field will be of assistance to others. Regarding your question, congrats on the big promotion—it sounds like the year ahead will be an exciting one for you. Teaching out of the country can be a bit tricky, but there a few items that can make it easier. First, remember the time zone differences; I've known many distance educators who vacationed out of the country, forgot the time zone differences, and missed important all-faculty webinars or student presentations they were to do. (Often, watches and smartphones have world clocks on them to keep you on top of the time, and you ought to set alarms to remind you of important deadlines.)

If you need make any calls from out of the country, nearly all major phone companies have special plans where you can have a limited amount of minutes that allow you to call from out of major countries. (I don't know the cities you'll be visiting—check with your phone provider.) Regarding ongoing interaction with your students, such as e-mails, class announcements, and feedback on assignments, it is your call as to whether you want students to know you are out of the country. But I'll give you my two cents here: minimize, if not totally eliminate, your being out of the country, as it can be a distraction for the students. (There is an exception: you are teaching accounting, and what you experience with a different country's accounting practices might prove valuable to your students. In this case, your letting them know about being out of the country stands to enrich your course!) Finally, be sure you have a strong and reliable Internet connection—and that you bring a converter that allows you to use another country's wall socket. Best of success in your new adventure!

My question is one I know you've discussed in several columns, on several different subjects, but it's one I believe that can always use more input: making my class more inviting to my students. Certainly, I have the options of using different-colored fonts and highlighting, as well as changing the size of my fonts, and I try to use language that just reads more inviting. Yet I know there must be more I can do—does your experience offer any tips in this area?

Student engagement is the #1 concern of distance learning educators, and I have written several columns directly or indirectly focused on this subject. There is a variety of items that can be done in a classroom to make it more inviting—you've touched on one, the look of your text through size, color, and style of fonts. But also your language is critical—not only must it be uplifting but also somewhat "cool," that is, you don't want to come across as a staid academic, as there is nothing interesting about this type of writing. But writing that is more conversational in tone (you do mention this!) and always is motivating and looks to help students is more interesting. Also, if you have the option of using videos—making your own or posting others—that highlight different subject areas of the course and relates the course to the "real world," do this! The visual, especially if it moves, keeps students involved. Of course, the use of cartoons, creating puzzles, and writing mini rap songs—all relating to your course (and if allowed by your school)—also makes a course more tantalizing. Finally: keep doing outreach—individual e-mails and, if acceptable, calls; these really will help you connect to the students ... and make your course more inviting!

Errol, your columns have been a boon for our department, but I've always been curious about one item you've mentioned several times: connecting courses to the world of work. I can think of an easy way to do this: simply mentioning how a course, for example, physics (which I teach), is important in a job setting (which I do). But I know there must be a whole "bunch" of other ways to do this. Would you share, please? Thank you!

Tying the course into that "real world" is crucial, for it makes the course much more than something merely academic and only good for a grade. And once this is successfully done, students react very positively to it. You are doing one of the keys: reminding the students of how a course ties into the job setting. Beyond this, here are a few other suggestions: (1) In a discussion thread ask students to share how the course or a subject in the course relates to their goals/their work—students enjoy talking about themselves, and this gets them more active and reminds them of the tie-in. (2) When possible, include photos, stories, and video clips of the professional world where the knowledge of your course becomes crucial—this immediately reminds students that the course extends far beyond X number of weeks. (3) Creating a PowerPoint or a similar presentation with a focus specifically on the course's relation to the job market allows you to structure the connection exactly as you'd like it—and the colors and slides are fun for students. (Too, if the capability in your classroom exists, create videos with the same focus.) (4) Include quotes from folks in an industry that explain or mention the importance of your course subject in the world of work or the world in general. (5) Search your library for links to the employment scene, and remind students of these: while these may not be specific to your course subject they do remind students of the school's tie-in to the professional scene. Use one or more of these suggestions—they will make your students more interested in your course! (And by the way: thanks so much for the pat on the back—I'm glad my columns are helping your faculty teach online!)

Remember: Executive chefs can be stars—but not so much without prep cooks, sous chefs, and kitchen assistants.

Volume 18, Number 3, 2018

Quarterly Review

OF Distance

Education

RESEARCH THAT GUIDES PRACTICE

Editors:
Michael Simonson
Charles Schlosser

≡IAP
INFORMATION AGE
PUBLISHING

An Official Journal of the
Association for Educational Communications and Technology

QUARTERLY REVIEW OF DISTANCE EDUCATION,
SUBSCRIBE TODAY!
WWW.INFOAGEPUB.COM

4. There is an *instantaneous phenomenon* to social media. When instructors post, students receive, and vice-versa.
5. There is a needed match between *instructional design* and social media. If social interaction is a part of a course, a well-planned instructional design strategy is mandatory.
6. The *third party* is removed. Social media are if nothing else, personal. We do social media without the need for help, or supervision. The information technology professional's role in social media-based instruction is minimized.
7. Social media make instruction seem *friendly*. The whole basis of connecting and interacting is to be social. This works for education also.

Unfortunately, there seems to be a less positive side to the use of social media in online learning. Let's call these seven the seven distractions ("addiction" seems too strong a term). The seven distractions now being referred to in the literature as nomophobias (*no-mo*bile fears, get it?) are:

1. There is a *greediness* dimension to the use of social media. In other words, users want likes and expect repeated and rapid interaction.
2. *Gluttony* is another of the cons of social media in online learning. There is a need to know everything related to what is being examined and discussed.
3. There is a level of *lustfulness* when social media are used. I want this or that or everything. These three deadly sins—greed, gluttony, and lust—are related and harmful in the extreme.

4. *Pleasure seeking* is a documented consequence of social media use. Learners look for what makes them happy and contented, and this is often not what instructors want. Education must sometimes hurt a little.
5. Some *students are afraid* of social media uses in online instruction. They do not want to interact so often or in the level of detail that others in their class might want. Research shows that if someone is positive in social media, readers perceive this as neutral, and neutral responses are perceived as negative. Truly negative interactions are ego shattering for some.
6. Unfortunately, instructional design, while important and even critical in any online instruction, is often ignored when social media are used. Social media are so easy that *systematic planning is often ignored*.
7. *Feeling left out* happens. If instructors and classmates do not respond in the manner of social media users, some wonder what has happened, or what did I do, or what did I miss.

How do we decide if social media applications have a place in online instruction? The answer is simple; there is no choice, students have already decided. The real key is how distance educators harness the positives and reduce the negatives.

And finally, as Johnny Mercer and the Pied Papers sang "accentuate the positive, eliminate the negative, latch on to the affirmative, don't mess with Mister In-Between."

Social Media and Online Learning
Pros and Cons

Michael Simonson

"Social media are cool. I have 325 Facebook friends."

Are social media applications empowering or addicting—or both?

Certainly, social media provide a type of interaction and connectivity that was unheard of a few years ago. In the modern distance education era, the quest for interaction and connectivity has been a hallmark of well-designed online learning, and social media applications seem to provide a needed and desirable dimension to online instruction. But it seems that there are pros and cons to the use of social media applications in teaching—empowerments and additions.

Seven positive consequences of social media when used in online instruction come to mind and these seven might be referred to as *the seven empowerments*.

1. Social media are *cool*. Sites like Facebook and Twitter give the impression of being modern, so classes that have a social media dimension are perceived as new and generational.
2. Social media promote the *ego syndrome* of users. We can access information about our classmates, and they can do the same. Teamwork is promoted.
3. Social media promote *self-education*—users can find out what they want quickly and this can expedite the teaching and learning process.

... continues on page 71

Michael Simonson, Editor, *Distance Learning*, and Program Professor, Programs in Instructional Technology and Distance Education, Fischler School of Education, Nova Southeastern University, 3301 College Avenue, Fort Lauderdale, FL 33314. Telephone: (954) 262-8563. E-mail: simsmich@nsu.nova.edu

CPSIA information can be obtained
at www.ICGtesting.com
Printed in the USA
FFOW01n1431180618
47172019-49818FF

9 781641 132831